THE ANGELS
IN RELIGION AND ART

Other Books by Valentine Long, O. F. M.

Not on Bread Alone

They Have Seen His Star

Magnificent Man

Fountain of Living Waters

Bernadette and Her Lady of Glory (paperback)

Whatever Comes to Mind

THE ANGELS
IN RELIGION AND ART

by №00001
VALENTINE LONG, O.F.M.

FRANCISCAN HERALD PRESS / Chicago, Illinois

Imprimi potest:

Cronan Kelly, O. F. M.

Vicar Provincial

Nihil obstat:

John J. Manning, O. F. M.

Censor Deputatus

Imprimatur:

✝ Lawrence B. Casey

Bishop of Paterson

April 6, 1970

Except where otherwise noted, the Scriptural quotations in this book are from the Revised Standard Version of the Bible, copyright © 1946 and 1952, by the Division of Christian Education of the National Council of the Churches of Christ in the U. S. A., and are used with permission.

The author also wishes to thank the publishers listed below for permitting him to quote from the works indicated. The folios in parentheses indicate the pages in this book on which the quotations are to be found: Random House, Inc., New York, Dante's *The Divine Comedy,* translated by Lawrence Grant White, copyright © 1948, by Pantheon Books, Inc. (pp. 2, 21, 141, 193, 194, 195, 196, 197, 198, 199); Chappell and Co., Inc., New York, Cole Porter, "True Love," copyright © 1955 and 1956 (p. 8); A Watkins, Inc., New York, *The Comedy of Dante Alighieri, Purgatory,* Vol. II, translated by Dorothy Sayers, copyright © 1955 (p. 1); Harcourt, Brace and World, Inc., New York, Dorothy Sayers, *The Nine Tailors,* copyright © 1934 by Dorothy Leigh Sayers Fleming; copyright © 1962 by Lloyds Bank, Ltd. (p. 158); Holt, Rinehart, and Winston, Inc., New York, Jacques Maritain, *The Peasant of the Garonne,* translated by Michael Cuddihy and Elizabeth Hughes, copyright © 1968 (pp. 15, 16).

Second Printing, 1971

PRINTED IN THE UNITED STATES OF AMERICA

FRANCISCAN HERALD PRESS, 1971

To the memory
of my beloved parents

CONTENTS

THE ANGELS
IN RELIGION AND ART

The Angel Is No Stranger

NOTHING BETTER proves the angel's appeal to the popular mind, and the ideal it cherishes of him, than the usual compliment that attributes to people of quality an angelic excellence.

"She sings like an angel," is what any choirmaster might say of his prize soprano. "When Dante is moved he writes like an angel," is what Dorothy Sayers has said of her favorite poet. "His physical beauty is astonishing," remarks Thomas Wolfe of Luke Gant, and then adds the main reason why: "His head was like that of a wild angel." From centuries of use the cliché slips naturally into place for Hamlet when he recounts the glories of man: "How noble in reason! How infinite in faculty! In form and moving how express and admirable! In action how like an angel!"

The gifted, in whatever capacity, invite the comparison. "He is merry like the angels who have never known the pains of earth," writes Somerset Maugham of a character of invincible charm, Alyosha Karamazov. "All who sat in the council," we read of St. Stephen on trial, "saw that his face was like the face of an angel."[1] What was it, again, that

---

[1] Acts 6:15.

1

Newman said of the saints? They "rise up from time to time in the Catholic Church like angels in disguise and shed around them a light as they walk on their way heavenward."

If the saint deserves the comparison above all others, it is the glamour girl who more often receives it. The first time that Beatrice addresses Dante in his great poem — and she is as much beauty queen as saint — he thrills to her radiance and to a clarity in her voice something like that of an angel:

> Her eyes were gleaming brighter than a star
> When she replied to me in accents mild,
> Her voice serene, and like an angel's clear.

A woman of charm who looks and talks like an angel may be expected in song after song to act like one. Recently on TV, not at all surprisingly, a comely comedienne, flanked by two admirers, set them a sprightly pace as the three ambled about to the accompaniment of their own voices. She chattered away at them, turning from one to the other, as one crooned into her right and the other into her left ear: that she did this and did that and everything else just the way an angel would do it. The boys had their minds fixed on the idea. Nor did the audience find it tiresome. The act brought the loudest applause of the hour.

In amatory verse, where feelings run high, simile yields easily to the more direct metaphor and then a Geraldine of the anthologies forthwith becomes "an angel in a frock." Lovers in song, more often than not, do not see in their fiancé or bride or even their unattainable dream girl a mere resemblance to an angel. Why beat about the bush? She *is* one. It would be interesting to count how many of our lyrical benedicts have married, on their own word, not daughters of men but angels of heaven.

The Shakespearean lover is second to none when it comes to discovering these "angels of heaven" on earth. "By Jupiter, an angel!" exclaims Belarius, recognizing Imogen for one instantly. Her boy's clothing does not for a moment conceal from him her celestiality. Nor, later, does her normal feminine apparel, her night garb, mislead Iachimo. "A heavenly angel," he says of her softly but with firm confidence as he stands looking upon the sleeping beauty. Then, of course, there is Romeo, whose Juliet has just spoken into the night from her balcony to stir in him an insatiable longing. "O speak again, bright angel!" he calls, ready to climb to her under the starry sky.

In classic verse, an impressive percentage of its angels are women in their twenties. To Keats, Madeline kneeling at her night prayers looked perfectly fit to assume the role of seraph. In his own wording:

> She seem'd a splendid angel, newly drest,
> Save wings, for heaven.

But age is not necessarily a determining factor. With fine indirection John Ashe describes a girl under ten who has just complained that "we meet no angels now":

> And soft lights streamed upon her;
> And with white hand she touched a bough;
> She did it that great honor —
> What! meet no angels!

But then, as the late Oliver St. John Gogarty has pointed out, how could she herself have known that she was one?

Meanwhile, what about the men? Have they been forgotten? Not really. It is rather a matter of having less to quote since the written acknowledgments of their angelic traits have come far more sparsely. Yet, in their measure, they have come.

> And they were happy — for to their
>   young eyes
> Each was an angel and earth Paradise.

There, obviously, Byron has young Haidée think her lover an angel quite as much as Don Juan thinks that she is one.

"For angelic wit I know not his fellow," Erasmus said of the man for all seasons. "A man so clearly on the side of the angels," Chesterton was found to be, that young Ronnie Knox at Oxford looked for no further recommendation but went right on reading him. And surely history has nominated St. Francis the seraph of Assisi, St. Bonaventure the seraphic doctor, St. Thomas Aquinas the angel of the schools. On a lower level, Charles Lamb saw in Coleridge "an archangel a little damaged." Of a great benefactor of the arts, John Butler Yeats wrote to his son, the poet, that "John Quinn is the nearest approach to an angel in my experience."

Yet the imbalance obtains. For every man who reminds people of an angel there are a hundred women who look the part. For every man or boy who is called one, there must be a thousand of the other sex so identified. Chivalry did not die with the Middle Ages. "They were veritable Angels of Mercy," Abraham Lincoln records of the Civil War nuns. "Fair sister of the seraphim" is the epithet reserved, in English classic verse, for Teresa of Avila. "The Angel in the House," in Coventry Patmore's long narrative poem by that name, refers to the poet's own wife, who inspired the effort. And Wordsworth, finding Mrs. Wordsworth "a perfect woman, nobly planned," notices about her as a final enhancement "something of angelic light." So in literature it goes.

In life, too. And a saint, of whom such angelizing of women seems a bit odd, furnishes a perfect example of it. At Turin, when he was dedicating its famous Marian shrine, Don Bosco saw to it that there were three distinct choral groups to give the music a resounding power. He had the first, an all-male choir, standing to one side of the sanctuary to represent the Church Militant as they sang of hope amid earthly distress. The second male choir on the opposite side of the sanctuary impersonated the Poor Souls, intoning the aspirations of purgatory. But the Angels of Paradise, not a male voice among the two hundred of them, occupied their given place in the exact center of things, directly under the massive dome, where in their celestial robes they trilled in high G of bliss unending. The favored group had not wrangled from the saint their distinction: it was his idea.

This penchant for angelizing women has become so much an obsession with writers, now and of the not too distant past, that in their delineations even the curls or bangs of a coiffure may turn out to be of an angelic fiber. Aldous Huxley (of whom it would hardly be expected) found something about the mere nose of Virginia Maunciple "that made you want to cry when you looked at it, it was so elegant and impertinent, so ridiculous and angelic." Dickens (of whom it would be expected) saw in Miss Wickfield's "an angel face." But then, as far as that goes, a current recording which sells well in the music shops ascribes to the object of its ravings a pair of "angel arms." A satirist himself does not escape the tyranny of the idiom. "When a young lady has angelic features," Stevenson allows, freely admitting that she has them, "she may be a little devil after all."

Even commercial advertising does not hesitate to capitalize on the angel's great popularity. Only recently, to cite an amusing instance, the slicker journals ran a full-page illustration of half a dozen girls wearing blouses of *Angel Skin,* as the texture is labeled. The models, to confirm its authenticity, each sport a becoming pair of wings with the same comic aplomb with which the nightclub bunny shows off her pointed rabbit ears, not to mention the tail.

Now, to be sure, using the angel to such a purpose would mean nothing if the thought of him did not command respect. His acceptability, if not as a person, then at least as a symbol of perfection, is everywhere taken for granted. His name gets into our very humor to sharpen it. And that affords another solid proof of his popularity.

James Thurber, to bring about the right, final twist to a situation, inserts a mention of the angels into his story "You Could Look It Up." The leading character, baseball manager Squawks Magrew, has been driven to a near fit of apoplexy by the misplays of an insufferable team when he switches his mind elsewhere just in time. "I wisht I was dead," comes the groan from the dugout. "I wisht I was in heaven with the angels."

This sudden jump of the mind to the sublime from the dreary brings with it a touch of mirth. It is what the mention of angels often does, to relieve the tensions of fiction, to sharpen its comedy. Faith in the angels brightens life. There is a song, usually heard on TV as a duet, in which the betrothed sing of a third party to their happiness with a smile in their voices: "You and I have a guardian angel on high with nothing to do but to give to us a love forever true."

An anecdote is told of a doctor and his diagnosis of a patient never seen before in his clinic.

"Tell me," said the doctor, "are you a smoker?"

"No, I am not."

"Do you drink?"

"Never."

"Do you possibly keep late hours with women?"

"No *possibly* about it! I don't!"

The doctor, reflecting, tried a new approach.

"Have you pains in the head?" he asked.

"In the head? No, not there — "

"That surprises me," mumbled the doctor, thinking to himself that the man's halo was fitting too tightly.

" — but I do have pains in the back," came the remainder of the reply.

"That's it!" blurted the doctor. "I knew I wasn't far off. You just haven't learned to fold in your wings when you sit down."

Naturally, as a taunt to the pietistic, all such jesting about growing wings presupposes the angel to be an exemplar of piety. His wings represent, in the popular notion, his unsullied innocence. They have served art from time out of mind as a convenient symbol of his holiness as well as his agility.

But the many infidels of the day consider the angel himself only a symbol. They admit his enormous prestige, having no choice but to concede it. Nor would they want to deprive the angel of this. They accept him on their terms as a respectable convenience, a necessity of make-believe, a fancied paragon with whom to compare, whereby to appraise, our human models of excellence. It was an agnostic, I think, who on the radio said of Winston Churchill that "he fights evil like an aroused archangel."

This habitual reference to the angel as a criterion of merit, from people of every shade of belief, indicates beyond a doubt his universal reputation. But there remain other and no less notable indications. Art, not to mention at present the religious liturgies, reflects in many a masterpiece the demand of the ages of faith. In response to that popular demand it has given the angel a wealth of attention.

Its memorials of him meet the curiosity of the tourist everywhere. In Moscow, merging into the skyline of the Kremlin, rises the dome of the city's noblest edifice, the Cathedral of the Archangel, a Byzantine attraction still intact, and still in possession of its precious icon of St. Michael the Warrior. In Bethlehem, or, rather, in the adjoining Shepherds' Field, stands the Chapel of the Angels that at Christmastide can scarcely accommodate its international influx of pilgrims. Rich in variety, the memorials range from the elaborate grandeur of the basilica to the simplicity of an isolated statue. In New York's Central Park, a sightseer who follows directions to the famed Bethesda Fountain will notice with a tug of joy a gigantic bronze angel surmounting the structure, cast in a swift but graceful walking stance, agleam in the sun, overshadowing the water, dominating all that immediate environment of sylvan charm.

But we needn't enter a park, or a church or museum, to see what an impact the angel has made on art. National postage stamps carry his image into homes everywhere on earth. Italy has put a stamp into use that reproduces Donatello's *Singing Angels*. The Grand Duchy of Luxembourg has one in circulation that features an orchestra of angels copied from a highly wrought column of its Cathedral of Notre Dame. The United States consecutively, for the Christmas season, issued stamps depicting, from three masterpieces of art, a solitary angel blowing his jubilant trumpet, a Madonna whose attendant angels could not be shown for lack of space but are known to belong there, and, finally, standing alone, the Gabriel of an Annunciation set.

Obviously, the strong national preference for these stamps during a season when the mails run heaviest cannot but prove the angel's popular appeal. He has had that proved in more ways than a few. The world traveler is not surprised that houses of worship bear such titles as Guardian Angel, St. Michael, St. Raphael, St. Gabriel, or Holy Angels. But the patronage does not stop at that. Bolivia has its San Miguel River, Paris its Boulevard St.-Michel, California its San Gabriel Mountains, Argentina its city of San Rafael, while the Azores have their Island of São Miguel, by far the most prominent in the archipelago. Geography confirms the angelic cult.

Under no consideration is the angel a stranger to the world. The publicity he has received from art, in the press, on radio and TV, has made him a familiar ideal to every segment of society. To the devout who foster his presence he is the most practical of ideals; he lives to them and on intimate terms with them. He fulfills their need of him. He is a cherished reality.

Some years ago when the White House was being redecorated, President Kennedy selected for his bedroom drapery, reports a close friend, "a deep blue *toile de Jouy* featuring a spate of cherubs in its design." And Mary Thayer tells why. "I've always loved angels," she quotes him as saying. A man of his upbringing, and loyal to it, naturally would so react to them. They were a doctrine of his faith.

They still are. They always will be. Their existence, let it be proudly acknowledged, is an eternal truth.

The Angel Has His Credentials

THE ANGEL, no stranger to the earliest records of mankind, remains nevertheless a good test of faith.

Our infidels deny him outright. But what does that prove? An extreme type of nihilist has even denied himself, arguing his own nonentity. Who, then, is doing the arguing? How, if he doesn't have it, can a person renounce existence? Common sense must always find it incredibly funny whenever, as Belloc has pointed out, a Professor Schmidt blandly announces: "I cannot help all I do. I have no will. And what is more, there is no Professor Schmidt."

Does the man himself believe that? Certainly his audience does not. What they see they rather think is there. What they have heard has made them laugh; they cannot rid themselves of the notion that the pronouncement issued from what looked to be a mouth. We can imagine, from the set mannerisms of any public speaker, the roving glance this one turns upon his audience. He is curious to know their reaction: this immediately betrays an amusing self-confidence on his part, an inner satisfaction with his own dear reality. His denial of Professor Schmidt does not convince.

"Seeing is believing" has always been an axiom of common sense. Yet, with all due allowance, what sane mind could possibly think that the eye was made to see everything? Who has ever noticed the deadly fumes of carbon monoxide? Or scented them? Can we sniff or see a thought? Do we really see the air while seeing through it? Is the rainbow discredited because the color-blind cannot distinguish its shining hues?

Some truths, most truths, the supreme truths, do not rely on the senses for their credibility. In philosophy our greatest thinkers, and in literature our greatest poets, have acknowledged the spiritual world. They have but voiced the conviction of mankind at large. The village atheist has until modern times stood out, as the phrase connotes — an amusing oddity. If today his singularity has been lost in the current welter of unbelief, the fact remains that the Bible outsells by a wide margin all other publications. It retains the distinction of being, in an overcrowded market, The Book. No materialistic classic deserves mention with it. The Bible enjoys a renown unmatched.

What conclusion is to be drawn? The strong materialism that marks our age may not be denied. But neither may this: a generation so intent on the divine record, which tells of a greater unseen world in relation to ours, proves that it has not grown indifferent to God and his angels. If it had, why would there be so many discussions about him, so many popular references to them?

That an intense look at the heavens cannot bring a single angel into view does not mean that the angels are not there. Nor again, that they are. It proves neither. It leaves the question open to other avenues of information than the senses.

Angels owe their credibility, for those who believe in them, to divine revelation. Once admit the Bible to be of God, to be his vehicle of communication with man, and the admission ought to include its angels. What would we think of an astronomer who admitted the firmament to the exclusion of its stars? Well, with just such relevancy do the angels belong to Scripture.

St. Paul could not have expressed a higher opinion of angels than when he warned the Galatians of the false prophets in their midst, who were perverting the doctrines of divine revelation. "Even if we," he writes, "or an angel from heaven, should preach to you a gospel contrary to that which we preached to you, let him be accursed."[1] No angel of heaven would ever do that, being an angel: but supposing he did, the apostle argues, do not be taken in, resist him as an evil agent, withstand the effrontery of his misused power, do not be intimidated into error by his grandeur of person.

The angels themselves, to certain avant-garde theologians, have become a prime target of abuse. They have the best of company: God himself has not escaped the abuse. It grieves Jacques Maritain, and infuriates him, that, where least expected, such an epidemic of error should have broken out. He has a harsh name for its proponents, calling them "public relations men of the Old Liar." Nor does he miss the bitter humor of the fact that, having lost faith in the angel, they have lost faith in the devil.

They have beyond a doubt confused the faith of many who were foolish enough to take them seriously. But, as the aggrieved old peasant of the Garonne has indicated, we were long ago forewarned. "The time is coming," reads the text in question, "when people will not endure sound teaching, but having itching ears they will accumulate for themselves teachers to suit their own likings, and will turn away from listening to the truth and wander into myths."[2]

Maritain does not think that the current distortions, however rampant, will prevail. Nevertheless, for the present they are a disturbance, and he does not choose to ignore them. He reserves perhaps his keenest barbs for those of the contemporary Biblical scholars who have made themselves, to their own

---

[2] 2 Tim. 4:3.

evident satisfaction, "studious expurgators of the revealed truths." They clearly do not share his veneration of God's holy angels. When these strange exegetes have done with them, they are no longer the glorious beings who, on the word of Christ, behold the face of his Father in heaven, but are rather mere survivors of Babylonian imagery. They have been reduced to fanciful symbols. They have no more reality than a metaphor.

Why, one should like to know, would a Biblicist labor so assiduously to twist meanings out of words that to plain common sense are not there? Whatever the answer with its implications, let it go unsaid. What shall be said is that the solid tradition of the centuries, the combined testimony of the Synagogue and the Church, stands opposed to such extravagant sophistry. It affirms the angels. It does not disown our spiritual cousins. It believes they are a revealed truth of God, not subject to change, though open to the investigation of fresh insights which, if genuine, do not destroy but strengthen.

The doctrine that angels exist and are persons, not an imagination, could not have been more solemnly ratified. In 1215 the Fourth Lateran Council decreed that "God by his infinite power created from the beginning of time both the spiritual and the corporeal creature, namely, the angelic and the mundane, and afterwards the human, a kind of intermediate creature composed of body and spirit." In

1869, in words to the same effect, the First Vatican Council reaffirmed the decree.

Neither Council was inventing. They both agreed with St. Paul that "all things were created, in heaven and on earth, visible and invisible, whether thrones or dominions or principalities or authorities."[3] Now don't you think it would take a wild mentality to infer from his direct mention of four distinct kinds of angels, that the apostle considered them unreal? Yet the inference has been attempted. And again it has been rebuked. Pope Paul, in his Creed of the People of God, lest they be misled, has included in his vigorous summation of faith an acknowledgment of "the pure spirits known as angels." Almost two decades earlier, in the courageous encyclical *Humani Generis,* Pope Pius XII took sharply to task those rash innovators who "question whether angels are personal beings."

Christ the Lord does not question whether they are. He speaks right out of their being responsible, intelligent witnesses. "I tell you," he declares, "every one who acknowledges me before men, the Son of Man also will acknowledge before the angels of God."[4] Whenever the Lord introduces a statement with his authoritative "I tell you," he is but emphasizing its extreme importance. "I tell you," once

---

[3] Col. 1:16.

[4] Luke 12:8.

again he says of these superior beings, "there is joy among the angels of God over one sinner who repents."[5]

Scripture likes to associate us with the angels, whom it always treats as persons. St. Paul had no doubt of their being aware, in the way people are, of his co-workers who, he writes, had become with him, "a spectacle to the world, to angels and to men."[6] The prophet Daniel knew from whom the three young men in the fiery furnace derived their protection. "The angel of the Lord," he explains, "came down into the furnace to be with Azariah and his companions, and drove the fiery flame out of the furnace, and made the midst of the furnace like a moist whistling wind, so that the fire did not touch them at all or hurt or trouble them."[7] "Because you have made the Lord your refuge . . . , no evil shall befall you," announces the Psalmist. "For he will give his angels charge of you to guard you in all your ways."[8]

If all its angels were deleted from Scripture, the reader would see from the void how necessary they are to the sacred text. They belong there. They play too impressive a part in the divine story, exert too strong an influence at its more critical moments,

---

[5] *Ibid.* 15:10.

[6] 1 Cor. 4:9.

[7] Dan. 3:26-27.

[8] Ps. 91 (90):9, 10, 11.

to be passed off as only incidental to it. They come into the recorded scenes as visitors who are not strangers. Their appearances, far from ever disrupting the narrative, fit into it and heighten its meaning. An exact count of the angels in both Old and New Testaments would alone suffice to establish their importance to divine revelation.

Would a count be possible, though? Their numbers would surely defy the attempt; not the individual apparitions, abundant as they are; but such multitudes as crowded the visions of prophets or sang to the shepherds on Christmas night. To attempt a count would be to court failure. One might better try to enumerate a mob than a flight of angels.

Their legions, we have his own word for it, were ever available to Christ. "Do you think," he reassured a group of worried followers, "that I cannot appeal to my Father, and he will at once send me more than twelve legions of angels?"[9] Events from his earthly life verify the claim. During the Agony in the Garden "there appeared to him an angel from heaven, strengthening him."[10] After he had repulsed Satan, who had with characteristic cunning tempted him, "behold, angels came and ministered to him."[11] They moved in and out of his human life with a readiness that indicates their con-

---

9 Matt. 26:53.
10 Luke 22:43.
11 Matt. 4:11.

stant awareness of, their eager concern for, his earthly presence.

Not that they are reported to have come to him often; it wasn't necessary; the profound but matter-of-fact intimacy with which Jesus accepted their every recorded visitation to him implies a continuous availability. His followers seem to have understood this. On one occasion when he was addressing aloud his Father in heaven and a voice from the sky replied, some of his disciples concluded: "An angel has spoken to him."[12] All in all, except to the mind bent on explaining away the words, the Gospels have made it abundantly clear: that the angels were a familiar reality to Christ, and in their way as dear to him as the apostles. Faith in him, to be complete, must embrace them.

Art, as we have inherited it from the centuries, has surely taken to them. Without its many angels it would be missing an irreplaceable enrichment. Their being thus honored does not surprise. How on earth could it? The faith that has inspired the best of traditional art would by that very token have encouraged a generous treatment of such great favorites of Christ.

Every department of art has done the angels proud. Oratorios sing of them. Epics acclaim them. Sculpture has molded, painting has worked, into

---

[12] John 12:29.

human shape of transcendent charm their ethereality. Their representations show an effort that ranges from the master's technique to none at all: the demand has hurried the supply in favor of quantity, to the disadvantage of quality. One cannot look around an ordinary cemetery without noticing the usual marble or granite wings hovering above the memorials. Even Forest Lawn, which spurns the cross, has its angels.

We take their portrayals for granted, so used to them have we become, wherever we find them. Imagine the irreparable loss to *The Divine Comedy* if, by an impossible act of animosity, a materialist were to shoot down all its high-flying angels. It would require an arsenal of ammunition. In a single glance Dante saw, with their wings outspread, "countless thousands of rejoicing angels." For that matter, from the same urge of faith, Shakespeare has his Horatio invite whole flights of angels to sing Prince Hamlet to an eternal rest.

Naturalistic fiction itself, when it needs a symbol of pure beauty to offset the squalor of life, always knows where to find one. It goes to theology. It brings in the angel. And this rather adds to his credentials. It gives the argument for him a new dimension.

Look Homeward, Angel, a novel that has taken its title from *Lycidas,* like Milton cannot leave the subject alone. Its Oliver Gant, try as he would, "never learned to carve an angel's head" to satisfy his ideal of what it ought to be. Such beauty transcended the stonecutter's ability, but not his ambition. It obsessed him.

Angels have become an established familiarity to our culture. Even now, when that culture is in decline, they remain an interest. We are thereby the richer. And a study of them, who they are, what their nature is, their role in eternity, their place in the universe, their influence on history, their prevalence in art: all this, as gathered from Holy Writ and theology and the accounts of authentic visionaries, should not be held in contempt. The angels mean so very much to the human race. They deserve attention.

Some time ago a national celebrity being interviewed for *TV Guide* came out flatly with the statement that she believes in flying saucers. "It's presumptuous to believe," she gave for her reason, "that God only created us." By this I suppose she meant that he has put other intelligent beings than men into creation. He positively did. Only, the name for them is *angels*.

III

Who the Angel Is

THE ANGEL, to a faithful reader of the Bible, requires no introduction. There remains, however, a complementary source of information: the vast reserve of theology. Following the undeveloped leads of Holy Writ, theology has filled in the gaps so as to give to the angel a complete identification.

He has been defined as a creature who for sheer excellence comes nearest to God; a spirit, although he may for his purpose assume a human form; a person without sex, although grammar has assigned to him the masculine gender and art portrays him as of either sex. The angel, it may reasonably be said, is a no-body of tremendous importance.

There are those, let it be added for what it is worth, who resent the grammarian's dictate that the angel belongs irrevocably to the masculine gender. To them, this smacks of an untoward partiality which the universal custom of likening every beautiful girl to an angel does not amend. Nor do all the dissenters keep their resentment pent in. Some speak out. But this, in a world numbering more women than men, might be expected.

Expected or not, it occurs. In a large parish church when the sacrament of Confirmation was being administered, and it came her turn, a young girl who had her mind set on Michael for a name was told that, strictly, this was not a girl's name.

"Neither is it a boy's," she retorted softly, with a smile to the bishop.

She received the name.

Not having a body, the angel cannot help being a mystery to man. Yet by no dictate of human experience does his immateriality disprove his existence. That we cannot stare an angel into view, though he sees us, simply argues a shortcoming on our part. His invisibility excludes him only from our vision, not from life, the faithful believe. Do we see God, either? Has anyone ever had a look at his aspirations?

We take it on faith from the chemist that the surrounding air, without which we could not survive the hour, constitutes a blend of nitrogen and oxygen and hydrogen. The eye can discern nothing of it; but on the authority of science the mind accepts the mystery. What science cannot do, however, is something of far greater import: it cannot analyze a spirit, it cannot demonstrate an immateriality. Belief in the angel comes from divine revelation.

Apologetics, intent on establishing the authenticity of divine revelation and the corresponding reasonableness in accepting it, has had elaborate treatment from many a reliable and, on occasion, brilliant pen. *Theology and Sanity,* devoting three chapters to the angels, good and bad, has all the wit of F. J. Sheed behind its argument for their existence in the general vindication of the Faith. *The Case for Christianity,* in the crystal-clear style of C. S. Lewis, states the case with not a wasted word. There never was a more succinct analysis of evil than the summary in this book, which concludes: "And do you now begin to see why Christianity has always said that the devil is a fallen angel?"

Lewis himself cannot see how anyone who believes in Scripture does not believe in both the angels of heaven and the angels of hell. "I believe in angels," he writes in his racy preface to *The Screwtape Letters and Screwtape Proposes a Toast,* "and I believe that some of these, by the abuse of their free will, have become enemies of God and, as a corollary, to us."

What does it mean when theology says that the angel is a pure spirit? It means that he is a being inaccessible to our senses; his is a nature without physical shape, and when he assumes a form it is not of his essence; he is a compound of sheer intelligence and will. Man, accordingly, may not be called a pure spirit: the soul animating his body is confined to it, depends on it. Free of any such confinement, of any such interdependence, the angel has nothing of the kind to restrict his movements. He is all spirit, "the most excellent of creatures because he bears the strongest resemblance to God," reflecting best God's beauty and holiness and majesty. So teaches St. Thomas Aquinas, who once enjoyed the direct experience of an angelic apparition.

Being a pure spirit, the angel is never a weakling. He takes no half measures. He is forthright. He cannot hesitate. Everything he does has behind it the full and instant energy of his powerful will. Thus did Satan under trial, in choosing wrongly, do it with the unalterable decisiveness of his nature. A fallen angel never repents. A blessed angel, having made up his mind once and for all, can never sin.

The angel, not being divine, does not enjoy ubiquity. But of all creatures he comes nearest to it. He gets around with a speed that would embarrass an airliner. A New Yorker in a hurry to get to Los Angeles could not do better than take a jet. An angel could make the same flight without having to ride a vehicle, while the New Yorker was fastening his seat belt. He could so outspeed a CBS telecast from coast to coast that while the program was just leaving New York, he would have arrived in Los Angeles.

He could arrive in the city of his name, from whatever distance, the moment he wanted to be there. He moves at will.

An angel's flight, to cite an exact analogy, enjoys the speed of thought. It would come easy to a dreamer sitting in his prison cell to think of Bermuda, its sun bathers and sand dunes, all in a single instant. It would require no acrobatic ingenuity for his mind the very next moment to jump to the moon and the moment after that to plunge deep into the ocean to enter a submarine bedded there. Matter cannot resist thought. It cannot control the spiritual. It cannot impede the angel.

Space throws up no barriers to his flight. Nothing within the wide limits of his created power can restrict him. It is inconceivable that, having no body, he could be locked in jail. He could, however, break into one. St. Peter discovered that.[1] And had the apostle been confined to a steel vault instead of a cell, it would have made no difference. The angel would have got in, to direct the escape.

A spirit of his purity, reasons the *Summa,* "is where he acts and is instantaneously present where he decides to be." An angel, exerting his power on our material world, does it by the providence of God. He can do it, now here, now there, anywhere at all. How far apart the points of action, does not concern him. Distance to him is no problem.

His intellect, matching his prodigious force of will, understands with unerring accuracy the universe. Think of the centuries of laborious striving

---

[1] See Acts 12:7.

on the part of astronomy to accumulate its fragmentary information, and then consider this: the angel knew it all from his beginning, and all that astronomy has still to learn. He does not by means of a telescope have to compute the vast reaches of interstellar activity. He suffers no pangs of frustration. He has no regret that, having done his best, trillions of unattainable stars remain outside his calculations. He already has their number.

One of our astronauts to outer space said that it was roomy enough there for both angels and men. He was one of the Apollo 8 Mission which radioed to earth the opening verses of Genesis while encircling the moon. A man of faith, he knew that the astronauts had not had this stretch of outer space to themselves and that the angels could fly there without instruction. Elaborate planning is not a prerequisite of the angel.

Where did this mighty intellectual obtain his schooling? Forget the question. Who of his kind needed it? Research to him is nonsense. Created in full possession of his great natural endowments, the angel has had the mind to penetrate from the start the toughest secrets of science and to comprehend with the quickness of a glance the vast extent of the complicated universe.

This, however, only shows a lower level of his mentality. What secrets of the Divine Grandeur come to the angel from direct contemplation, giving him his highest knowledge, no theologian dare say. He doesn't know. "No eye has seen, nor ear heard, nor the heart of man conceived, what God has prepared for those who love him."[2]

The angel has a mind second only to God's. "Not even the angels of heaven," our blessed Lord said in praise of their acute intelligence, could know the exact day of judgment.[3] The implied meaning of this seems clear: if they do not know, who but God does?

And that leads to an important comment. From such telling statements of Christ, and the many other relevant statements of the Bible, does angelology gather its material to work on. It does not spin out mere fantasies. It is not guessing. Its deductions are solidly based on the word of God. It draws on the Old and New Testaments. It finds its clues for speculation in the sacred book.

Do you recall from your Old Testament how an angel of the Lord, seeing that Daniel sat hungry in the lions' den, hurried off to him a highly nutritious dinner? The incident bears witness to that tremendous force of will, that sharp vision of mind, which the theologians have inferentially ascribed to the angelic nature.

"Now the prophet Habakkuk," runs the text, "was in Judea. He had boiled pottage and had broken

---

[2] 1 Cor. 2:9.
[3] Matt. 24:36.

bread into a bowl, and was going into the field to take it to the reapers. But the angel of the Lord said to Habakkuk, 'Take the dinner which you have to Babylon, to Daniel, in the lions' den.' " The prophet, firmly clasping the large bowl, did not think he should take the reapers' dinner to somebody else in a place unknown to him.

"I have never seen Babylon," he excused himself, "and I know nothing about the den."

That did it! There would be no further nonsense from the man. "The angel of the Lord took him by the crown of his head, and lifted him by his hair and set him down in Babylon, right over the den, with the rushing sound of the wind itself."[4]

Quick as a flash, Daniel had his meal. Within moments he was eating it, enjoying it.

What do you think of that, now, for catering service? What do you think of that as a demonstration of will power? As a display of discernment that knew from miles away Daniel's urgent need and the availability of Habakkuk to serve him? No precision instrument of the flying pilot could have more accurately indicated to the angel, who required none, the exact instant for descending upon the lions' den with his unusual luggage.

A clairvoyant with his extrasensory discernment, a Dante with his quick and penetrating insights, an Anna Catherine Emmerich with her astounding pre-

---

[4] Dan. 14:33-39.

monitions, may suggest ever so faintly some idea of angelic intuition. But no more than that! Neither human intelligence, nor human brawn, nor again human beauty, can at their natural best come remotely close to the angelic endowment. Alongside an angel, were the comparison possible, the smartest philosopher would seem rather a nitwit, the strongest athlete a weakling, the rarest model of feminine charm a sad disenchantment.

We may as well face it. Nature for nature, the angelic by every conceivable standard exceeds our own. It is the truth. But it is not, as a future chapter will show, our embarrassment.

IV

When the Angel Wears a Body

THE TEACHER WRITES the word on a blackboard. Her class of youngsters read it, letter by letter, a n g e l. And immediately, without hesitation, what takes place in their young minds? There immediately comes alive in them the picture of a beautifully enrobed human body with wings, hovering in midair.

Art has so conditioned those young minds. The children simply remember the picture from their reading book, as an illustration to the text. When they think of an angel, he has for them a human form with wings for flying around. They have come to associate the angel with a body he doesn't really have. Isn't that, of course, what we all do?

Art must give the angel a body, or leave the spirit alone. No painter of a Michelangelo's creativity could depict on his canvas an invisibility. But a genuine artist does not allow a mere impossibility like that to stop him: he uses his ingenuity to get around it. Nor yet does his embodying the spirit violate the truth. The angel's reality recommends it.

The arts have really adopted the idea from Scripture. How often in the sacred annals has not an angel taken bodily shape to appear to mortal eyes? He usually comes in the role of messenger. He ma-

terializes on the scene with startling instancy, to en-
lighten, to guide, to command, or to warn and rebuke. His apparition serves without fail some urgent
demand.

The scriptural angel, when described in human
form, is of masculine appearance. "There stood before me one having the appearance of a man," is
how the prophet Daniel describes the angel Gabriel.[1]
Tobias, requiring a companion for his hazardous
journey, turned into the road to find waiting for him
"Raphael who was an angel," but who looked like
Azarias.[2] "A young man," again, announced to the
women at the tomb the resurrection.[3] And the evangelist Matthew, by a master stroke of indirection,
suggests of his angel at the sepulchre, who rolled
back the stone, a vigorous physique. Radiant with
power, he unnerved the guards and sent them sprawling on their faces.[4]

The Bible relates rather than describes its angelic
apparitions. Of the angel who wafted Habakkuk to
the lions' den, what more than his action and words
do we have for gaining some notion of how he
looked? That he grabbed the prophet by the hair
of his head to whisk him off like a sack of straw,
suggests indeed a strong human body.

---

[1] Dan. 8:15.

[2] Tob. 5:4.

[3] Mark 16:5.

[4] See Matt. 28:2-4.

However, from the narrative this does not necessarily follow. An angel could speak and be heard without being seen; he could lift the heftiest prophet without having a hand to take hold of him. If electricity does not have to be seen in action to produce results, neither does a spirit. The angel who did off with Habakkuk could have remained bodiless, invisible as the wind, and still have carried out the errand.

When an angel appears in human form, his body is no more himself than are the clothes he also wears. It merely becomes for him the instrument to materialize his presence. It is an accommodation to his visionary. Disguising himself as a companionable youth, Raphael did not lose but was only adapting his ethereal superiority to the circumstances. In his own words to Tobias: "All these days I merely appeared to you and did not eat or drink, but you were seeing a vision. And now give thanks to God, for I am ascending to him who sent me."[5]

To other visionaries than those of Scripture, from the time St. John finished its final book to the present, God has sent his angels in bodily form. This we know from a reliable enough source. A number of the saints, thus favored, have said so. And the Church has believed them.

Need we accept their word? No, but their invariable reluctance to assert the claim, and then only

---

[5] Tob. 12:19-20.

after the pressure of duty would force them to it, does indeed favor its acceptability. So does a second consideration: the saints were not given to telling lies. But the strongest sanction comes of that unfailing grandeur of action which the genuine visionary has always shown after the charismatic experience. What better explanation do we have for Joan of Arc, for the ingenuity of her enormous daring, than her report that the Archangel Michael had appeared to her as a radiant warrior and that she simply followed his instructions along with those of St. Margaret and St. Catherine?

His embodiment, which is not actually the angel, does involve a mystery. What on earth does not?

The spoken word, transmitting a thought from one mind to another through the listening ear, affords a parallel. The utterance is not to be mistaken for the thought it conveys; they are distinct; left unspoken, the thought would remain no less a thought. What we hear in the spoken word is sound, what we read in the printed word are letters of the alphabet: yet the physical medium does suggest to the brain nonphysical ideas. Who can explain it? Who may deny it?

Do we not, to cite a second analogy, call a man's eyes the windows of his soul? Nor is it an idle phrase. Something of his spirit or personality does look out at us through his eyes. But it is no more to be identified with them than a word with the thought it expresses or an apparition with the angel whom it only represents. The principle behind all of this stands clear: when the immaterial reaches our senses through a material agent, neither loses its nature to the other. They do not merge.

If Raphael did not become the handsome young man he only appeared to be, neither did the human disguise become for that reason a deceitful untruth. On the contrary, it served the truth to complete advantage; got it across to young Tobias in the way he could best realize it; made it come alive to his senses. How better under the circumstances could heaven's solicitude, which is really the point at issue, have shown itself to him? His own response to his heavenly visitant holds the answer.

We might as reasonably accuse a looking glass of dishonesty as an angelic manifestation. For while no mortal eye has ever seen an angel in the full purity of his spirit, neither has any man seen his own face: what he beholds in a mirror is but its reflection. If from an impulse of dislike he should give the image a shattering blow, it would be his knuckles that bleed. The face wasn't there. Only its image was. But it appeared to be an infuriatingly honest one.

We trust our mirrors, having no doubt from their reflection how our faces look. Isn't it then understandable that a St. Joseph or a St. Joan, having the same intuitive confidence in their angelic apparitions, should have trusted them? They never felt deceived. Nor is there sufficient reason to think that they were.

An angel's beauty, to be sure, transcends our ability to sense even an apparition of it undimmed; so that the apparition, if it would not blind, must reflect so much and no more of the overpowering reality. St. Frances of Rome, when once an archangel shone on her with a force that made her eyes ache, had to divert her fascinated gaze from the intolerable charm of his face to the softer aura of light surrounding his human figure. As for the watchmen at Christ's tomb, either they never had a good look, or else had no look at all, at the angel whose radiance struck them down. The latter alternative seems the likelier. How exactly does one see what blinds him?

Scripture first attributed to the spirits of heaven a glory that outshines the sun. In no better way could it convey to us, who find our paragons of human beauty stunning enough, an angel's overpowering charm. Being creatures of sense, we speak of bright hopes or dark thoughts and bitter memories: but it is all fanciful talk. The immaterial can have neither color nor taste. Yet, to understand it as well as we may, sensory terms are needed. And the angel in apparition therefore adopts, as the best means to an end, a luminosity not unlike the sun's when he would express to mortal eyes his spiritual grandeur. This imparts to the visionary some idea of the truth.

His intelligence and will in perfect accord with God's give the angel his characteristic beauty. It is of an unimaginable charm. But nineteenth-century art, thinking to capture that charm as nearly as human effort possibly could, decided to womanize its angels. Every age follows its own trends, only to be ridiculed for them by the next. C. S. Lewis finds the Victorian angel an error of bad taste, avoiding the voluptuous solely by being so utterly insipid. Whether one agrees with so disdainful a criticism, the fact is that, to emphasize angelic beauty over angelic power, nineteenth-century art did make its typical angel into a model of womanly grace, clad in the long pleated gown then in fashion, showing off great coils of hair, a general delicacy of feature, and, to enhance all this, a set of neatly trimmed wings.

To be sure, the wings were no Victorian invention. Art had given the angel these ever since Isaiah reported his vision of the winged seraphim and Moses had taken instructions from the Lord God himself to "make two cherubim of gold" to surmount the Ark of the Covenant with their wings spread out.[6] In the inner sanctum of the Temple, moreover, were to stand guard two other cherubim, two giants fifteen feet tall, together having a wing-

---

[6] Ex. 25:18-20; see Isa. 6:2.

spread as wide as the sanctuary itself, reaching from the Ark in the center to the opposite walls.[7]

The divine script had called for wings. Plenty of them! And the Temple had them, not only in the sanctuary. The whole edifice looked alive with angels carved to the doors, to the walls, to the panels on the laver stands, even embroidered on the great curtain that hung at the entrance to the Holy of Holies. They all had wings.

When St. John reports that "I saw another angel flying in midheaven,"[8] while he does not mention wings, does he possibly suggest them? Does the statement of the prophet Daniel that the angel of his vision "came to me in swift flight"[9] also imply them? We cannot be certain.

What is certain from her own account is that St. Gemma Galgani's regular visitant from heaven wore wings. "I begged him to remain near me," she writes in her diary of a night when she was afraid to be alone. "I went to bed; after that he seemed to spread his wings and come over my head. In the morning he was still there."

Conchita Gonzalez, one of the reputed young visionaries of San Sebastian de Garabandal in Spain, has likewise written that the angel of their earlier visions had wings. At first glimpse, the children

[7] 2 Chron. 3:10-13.

[8] Rev. 14:6.

[9] Dan. 9:21.

already knew him to be an angel. Was it his wings that had given the four youngsters the idea?

John Keats once complained that "Philosophy will clip an angel's wings." The protest was entirely justified. Literalism has not that right. An angel's wings belong to our concept of the angel as a fit symbol of his lightning-like quickness, an appropriate aid to his fictitious body in getting around in a hurry. The literal-minded do not benefit reality by disallowing an imaginary means to a better understanding.

He was a confused homilist who recently stood in his pulpit to announce to his congregation that he was repudiating the angel because he could not in conscience accept the wings as genuine. Neither does anyone else. Not the symbol, but what it symbolizes, happens to be the point of faith. Nor yet does the symbol, any symbol, any more than a metaphor, serve a dishonest purpose. No doll was ever meant to deceive the child into believing it a real baby. And the child, unless mentally ill, knows it.

V

How the Angel Came About

DANTE OPENS CANTO XI of his *Purgatorio* on a high note of praise of the angels for being the nearest of creatures to God, and the dearest, since they are most like him. The poet was only repeating what St. Thomas Aquinas had said. He was expressing in his *terza rima* a conviction common to the ages of faith. And he was thereby nullifying in advance the glib assumption that, prior to Copernicus, the faithful believed the universe to have been created for man's sake alone.

That is an inexcusably false assumption. It betrays an ignorance of the Faith on two counts. Christian doctrine has always held that, first of all, creation renders glory to God. It further holds that, because of his superiority to man in the natural world, the angel enjoys a deeper appreciation of it and a closer relationship to it. We are secondary to him.

On this account, however, we needn't feel at all slighted. Our inferiority admits of a supernaturalizing that brings with it a share with the angels in their beatitude. Heaven is not reserved to them.

"Come, O blessed of my Father, inherit the kingdom prepared for you," is an invitation to mankind.[1]

Nor has the Lord, nor have his apostles and
evangelists, nor again the patriarchs and prophets
of the Old Law, withheld from us the divine information that the angels, far from begrudging to man
a share in their glorification, will on the contrary
help him to attain it. Knowing our weakness, they
have for it a ready solicitude. Their superiority does
not disdain. They are not competitors. They are
rather allies.

They are, that is, if we wish them to be. They
do not force their aid; we must invite it. There
is no nonsense about them, no false sentiment. They
rejoice over a sinner's repentance; they welcome
every newcomer into heaven; but the soul has had
to meet the requirements. God's angels respect, as
does he, the freedom of the human will. Heaven
does not coerce an entrance.

The truth of the matter has, moreover, another
side, and it is sinister: not all the angels want us
to go to heaven. Some would prevent it. These are
the devils of hell. The worst of haters, they were
not always so. None was created evil. Once there
were no bad, but only good angels.

They all came alive out of nothing from a creative act of God, untold myriads of them, individuals
of such beauty, spirits of such intelligence, such

---

[1] Matt. 25:34.

ardor, such power and joy and perfection, as to defy the imagination. They all contributed to a common harmony of purpose. There was yet no discord among them. This, on the authority of Scripture, the homilies of the Fathers, the decrees and recommendations of the Councils, the resources of theology, forms the introductory truth about the angels.

Much remains open to speculation. Divine revelation, telling enough to satisfy its purpose, does not determine the incidentals. It does not conclusively say, to begin with, *when* the angels sprang into existence. It leaves that to theology.

Theology has not shirked the challenge. It has, as to the time of angelic creation, its theories. They are, broadly, two in number. Each of them warrants respect. Neither amounts to an article of faith.

The first, a minority opinion, holds that the angels were created with the universe. Certain of the Fathers cite in its favor the statement of Genesis: "In the beginning God created the heavens and the earth."[2] They interpret *heavens* to mean, besides the firmament, the higher immaterial realm of the angels. St. Epiphanus has no doubt about it. Origen admits some hesitancy. And leaving aside the text altogether, St. Thomas Aquinas argues from the standpoint of sheer expediency. He thinks it appropriate and therefore inclines to the belief that, since

---

[2] Gen. 1:1.

the angels were to be so providentially involved with the universe, the two got their start at the same time.

Not at all, argues back the other side. "Even though the angels had a beginning," St. Ambrose states the argument, "they were already there when the world was made." The majority of theologians agree. They consider the opening chapter of Genesis an exclusive account of the material world, the cosmos, and restrict the word *heavens* to meaning the visible firmament alone. The term does not, they say, include the spirit world. Rather, they maintain from another text, that the angels must have antedated the universe, since they are reported there to have greeted the creation of the stars with a shout of joy.[3]

It is not a conclusive argument. The angels, with their quick, intuitive understanding, could have come into being with the firmament and have known at once and jubilantly admired every star in it. They could have arrived in creation praising it. The universe and the angels could have got started together, with the latter in full acclaim of its wonders. Their sense of appreciation does not require time in which to develop. It is instantaneous.

Neither side of the debate enjoys certitude. Neither position has disproved the other. The question remains open.

---

[3] Job 38:7 (according to the Septuagint).

What *has* been settled as a certitude of the Faith, verified in Scripture, and decreed by the Fourth Lateran Council, is this: whether or not the angels preceded the material world into existence, they did precede man. Satan had already fallen — a fact which presupposes a heaven of angels from which he defected — when the story of man opens. The story takes for granted the priority of the angels.

And from the moment they began to be, they were as many in number as they are now. They do not generate. They enjoyed a fullness of their nature instantly, which none of them had yet degraded. They did not have to develop, as an infant does. Having no bodies, being pure spirits, they had nothing that could grow. Whatever made up their natural angelhood was all there, complete, from the start. What they knew, they knew at once. Without forethought they recognized in their very act of becoming, of being, the necessity of a Creator whom it was as natural for them to acknowledge as it is for man to breathe. Their own derivative beauty, while enthralling them, suggested to them without hesitation the superiority of its infinite Source. There were no atheists among the angels.

Nor, as has been said, did their intellect excel their natural force of will. The tremendous power attributed to this or that angel in Scripture, although it may appear to us miraculous, need not have been. The angel who alone slew an army of one hundred and eighty-five thousand to save Jerusalem, was doing what he had the natural power to do.[4] If the astonishing feat takes on for us the dimensions of a miracle, as we read of it in Isaiah and again in Kings, it is because we are judging the superhuman might of the angelic nature by standards of our own.

Thus could the angels act as well as think, without hesitancy, without error of judgment, doing what they willed to do within the spacious confines of a perfect nature. They did not need to think out the answers. They had them.

But their Creator, having given them so much, would on condition give them more. He would offer them the grace that, should they decide to accept it, would lift them beyond the proudest reach of their superb nature into the supernatural realm of the Beatific Vision. Meaning exactly what? That their finite minds would behold the Infinite, see God direct, experience his unveiled loveliness, which by nature they could not do; and that, having once glimpsed it, they would be ever drawn to it in an ecstasy of desire for nothing else. The discovery would be for them an absolute love at first sight, a sudden intimacy never to diminish, a state of unending bliss that would remain insatiable while it fulfilled.

No angel now in heaven, despite his acute strength of mind, could have anticipated the ecstasy that

---

[4] See Isa. 37:36; 2 (4) Kings 19:35.

awaited him. Therein lay the test. It transcended his understanding. He had to choose on faith.

The Beatific Vision, open to their choice, could have been just as surely the reward of the evil spirits as of the good spirits. Sadly, it is not. They decided against it. They turned it down.

VI

Angels Who Became Devils

THE ANGELS, receiving life, saw through it to its Creator. They had among them no dullards. They were not retarded in their knowledge of God. They were all, it may be said of them, instant theologians.

They were also, the moment there existed a universe to appreciate, instant astronomers. Our telescopes, probing its vast reaches, can only pick out for us the less remote stars; so that what we have learned of the cosmos remains infinitesimal compared to the magnitude of our ignorance. But we must not ascribe to the angels our limitations. At a glance they comprehended it all.

Nothing of it eluded their discernment. Nothing of it, as they at once caught its divine hint, could do else than feed their admiration for its Infinite Cause. No sooner had its trillions of units flashed into being, luminaries of stupendous bulk, knowing and following their course at a variety of tremendous speeds — no sooner had this brilliant maze of spheres swung into their complicated harmony than these alert witnesses were praising God.

"When the stars were made," Scripture has the Creator himself confiding to Job, "all my angels praised me with a great voice."[1]

The wording, as there used, is of the Septuagint, the earliest Greek version of the Old Testament. The Latin Vulgate, retaining, of course, the same idea, expresses it figuratively. "All the sons of God," it says of the angels, "shouted for joy" over the magnificent display of the universe. In either version, it is God who does the speaking in a kind of boast to Job about his appreciative and noblest creatures.

The angels are spirits. They had no parents. They required no secondary agents to get them into existence. They burst into life straight from God as the immediate offspring of his creative love. Why shouldn't they, then, in so appropriate a figure of speech, be called his sons?

But a question remains. Why, if the angels had such a natural proximity to him, such a quick grasp of his adorability, did a large number of them turn away from God?

Theology, raising the question, has the answer. Having at their creation no experience of the Beatific Vision, knowing of it only on faith as we now know of it, the angels were under no more constraint than we are, since it was a grace that transcended their nature. Although the angelic nature

---

[1] Job 38:7.

outreaches ours beyond the human power to imagine, still it comes incomparably closer to our inferiority than to God's infinitude. Within the limits of so perfect a nature as theirs, it is true, they could not go wrong, could not err in judgment: but in a matter outside it, so immeasureably above it, they could. The evil spirits in fact did.

Their bountiful Creator had offered them, without urging it, a participation in his own superangelic glory. Coercion would have degraded their dignity. It would certainly have deprived their beatitude, had they but achieved it, of the final element that would complete it: a realization of having themselves by an act of the will earned it. There was accordingly no forcing of the will. The fallen angels had retained their freedom to reject.

If once they had tasted of the Beatific Vision, had got just one direct glimpse of Infinite Beauty, they would of their own fascinated desire have prolonged the glimpse to an unending gaze of ecstatic joy. They would never have wanted anything else. No lesser desire could have competed with so ultimate a craving now forever fulfilled. That is what heaven means.

One look at such Infinite Beauty, and resistance must become an utter impossibility. But that was their trouble: Satan and his self-satisfied followers decided not to take the look that would have given them — besides their great exterior knowledge of

God — an intimate experience of his unveiled grandeur. Fascinated by their own excellence, which admittedly ranks topmost in the natural order, they set their will against his: they refused his invitation. They resisted his desire for them to enlarge their capacity for joy to a superangelic fulfillment. Unable to anticipate what this would be like, having to approach it solely on faith, on the strength of a promise, they preferred their natural independence. They felt sufficient to themselves. They trapped themselves in their overweening self-conceit.

The argument, neatly developed by St. Thomas Aquinas, does not stop there. It takes on a deeper dimension. It adds, from the suggestions of patristic theology, another possible element in the motivation of the defecting angels. They had been given to understand, so the supposition goes, that lesser embodied spirits, to be known as men, would likewise be invited to the same supernatural destiny; and that, moreover, the Son of God himself would become incarnate of a human mother; which in turn would mean that the angels of the Beatific Vision would have to adore to the full capacity of their love a Member of the human race who was also a Member of the Holy Trinity.

That settled it! The unwilling among the angels had had more than their pride would take. The whole idea offended their false sense of superiority. They would not yield their self-sufficiency to a higher state of intercommunicative charity. They wanted no part of such an affiliation with the Most High; to be shared with glorified animals, One of whom they would even be expected to adore. It revolted them to a consuming hatred. They would go to hell first!

And they did. Nor is there a way out for them. Nor, equally, would they accept a way out if they could. John Milton, who should have known from Dante how to portray Satan without dignifying his vile perversity, at least understood to perfection his "unconquerable will," the irreversible pride of his strong mind, his unrelenting preference for hell once he had decided for it against heaven.

> Hail, horrors! hail,
> Infernal world! and thou, profoundest hell,
> Receive thy new possessor, one who brings
> A mind not to be changed by place or time.
> The mind is its own place, and in itself
> Can make a heaven of hell, a hell of heaven.
> What matter where, if I be still the same.

The poet, in having Satan so applaud the error of his decision and welcome the consequent miseries of hell, writes in full agreement with sacred philosophy. He understood well its principle: that once an angel makes up his mind, because of the power, the intensity, the unhampered simplicity of his nature, it stays made up. There is never a reversal.

And that long speech from Satan, when the arch-fiend takes over the infernal Kingdom of Pande-monium, an acceptance speech which a fellow devil only interrupts to reinforce, reaches its summation in the famous passage which tells the whole story of their fixed impenitence:

> And in my choice
> To reign is worth ambition, though in hell.
> Better to reign in hell than serve in heaven.

The implication of cruelty which the usual refer-ence to hell is nowadays prone to attribute to God, is really a sentimental misunderstanding of the facts. No angelic spirit, no human soul, now there, had to go there. Not one of the damned but has loved self to the exclusion of God, and with an intensity that generates hatred of God the moment God's supremacy is recognized and has to be admitted. Those in hell would not exchange it for heaven, since to them hell is the miserable satisfaction of having forever their own perverse way. To be ab-sorbed in the unfathomable bliss of sharing with God his infinite grandeur, which is what heaven means, would be to his insatiable haters a worse torment than hell itself.

It is their attitude that creates the torment. Mil-ton, understanding this, got off a profound state-ment when he made Satan assert as a boast: "Myself am hell." This total egotism by its very nature shuts out God, who had intended the reprobates to be happy with him, but who would not force himself upon them. Their decision, equivalent to a demand, drew from him the curse of damnation.

"Depart from me, you cursed, into the eternal fire prepared for the devil and his angels,"[2] are words that clearly imply the double penalty of hell, the sense of loss, and the sense of pain. Of the two, every authority agrees, the essential torment to the damned is their disassociation from the Source of their being, whose rejected love they need more desperately than birds need air or fishes the sea. It is true, somewhat as it is true of the vice-ridden on earth, that the evil spirits have got what they want even while it sickens them. But that, rather than lessening, deepens their self-centered, God-forsaken misery. They must endure in their loss of God an eternity of frustration.

As to the other, secondary affliction, that of fire, the more literal-minded theologians consider it a mysterious kind that yet burns like a corporeal fire. They are of the opinion that this burning fire was something added to the dreadful loss of God to aggravate the torment. Others, understanding the word in a transferred sense, interpret it to mean the fury of hate that rages with no hope of relief in the spirits of the damned. Their misery, accordingly, is entirely of their own doing.

---

[2] Matt. 25:41.

The late Ronald Knox quite agrees. "Doesn't the loss of God," he asks in regard to the damned, "bring with it automatically the pain of sense?" The first, he thinks, implies the other. With less finesse but more vividly, the quotable schoolboy has given utterance to the same view. "Hell," he replied to his religion teacher, "is where God ain't and that's what burns you up."

St. Thomas Aquinas takes his stand halfway between the two positions. To him there is a distinct reality about hell fire, but not as an infliction of sensible pain, only as a confining encirclement of mental effect. Here are his words from the *Summa:* "The fire of hell does not actually cause the pain of burning, but it does torment the devil and the other damned spirits by the fact that it is constantly present; each spirit feels that it is surrounded by fire on every side, as if it were, so to speak, in a burning house from which there was no escape."

That the sufferings of hell should include sensible pain many a reliable theologian does not think feasible of spirits. This does not discredit the theologians' orthodoxy. The Church has never so decreed. She does indeed insist on the "unquenchable fire" which Scripture identifies with hell, as a doctrine of faith.[3] But its exact nature she has left

---

[3] Matt. 3:12; 13:41-42; 18:8-9; 25:41; Mark 9:43-48; Luke 16:22-24; Rev. 20:9-10; 20:15; 21:8; Ps. 21 (20):9; Judith 16:17; Isa. 33:14; 66:24.

open to speculation. And one of her great mystics, St. Catherine of Genoa, did not hesitate to give an opinion that follows the nonphysical interpretation and must surely exonerate the All-Just from the mistaken charge of cruelty. "The fire of hell," she has said, "is simply the light of God as experienced by those who reject it."

Just when the fall of Satan and his rebel angels occurred, or how long for the angels in general their term of probation lasted, is not known. With their kind of minds, quick to take in a situation, the trial could have come and gone in an instant. It may, on the other hand, have covered a period of time. We have not been told.

What Scripture does say about the fall is that it was Michael the Archangel, as God's voluntary avenger, who fought off the vain attempt of Satan to usurp a supremacy altogether impossible to him. The very names of the two, reflecting their opposite attitudes, indicate for us the situation. "Michael," a Hebrew derivative, which takes on the form of a question, and a challenging question at that, means "Who Is Like God?" whereas "Satan," another Hebraic term, means "The Adversary." Once fallen, the devil of devils opposed with all the hateful fury of his angelic power whatever is of God, whatever is good, whatever aids the heavenly destiny of man.

St. John, in his Biblical vision, saw Satan as a horrible dragon whose tail dragged along with it "a third of the stars of heaven."[4] The symbolism here has been interpreted to mean that one third of all the angels followed Satan to his downfall. That downfall was quick. Michael and his warriors stood for none of Satan's outrageous nonsense. Our Lord told his disciples, alluding to the event, "I saw Satan fall like lightning from heaven."[5]

The heaven there referred to is not the heaven of the Beatific Vision. It means a lower one, from which the rebel angels fell, and from which the loyal angels have now graduated to that highest of the different heavens spoken of in Scripture. St. Paul alludes to it. "I know a man in Christ," he writes of himself, "who fourteen years ago was caught up to the third heaven."[6]

The apostle had been given a glimpse into paradise, the supreme heaven, the realm of the Beatific Vision. He saw only enough to understand that what awaits the heaven-bound among us exceeds our brightest guess. Not an angel of God, incidentally, but desires us there. Not a devil of hell but desires our damnation.

---

[4] Rev. 12:4.

[5] Luke 10:18.

[6] 2 Cor. 12:2.

VII

Angels of Hate

THE FALLEN ANGELS hate us with an insatiable fury we cannot match, for in their downfall they retained the vehement intensity of a superior nature. That such enemies of man exist, faith in divine revelation may not deny. Turn where you will in your Bible, turn to the first pages, and the animosity of hell already shows there in the action of its arch-representative.

What is the story of Eve if not, along with its creational account, an implicit warning? Whether you interpret the story literally, as it used to be interpreted, or symbolically, as it is more likely now to be interpreted, its meaning comes out the same. The tragedy of it brings to a point our human liability to be taken in: an ironic naïveté which does not suspect in Satan the crafty malevolence that is surely there.

The evil spirits never find it easier to influence the human mind than when it considers itself immune to their malice; or, worse still, discredits the very existence of the evil spirits. If Scripture begins with a warning, it keeps up the warning throughout its many books, to the end. Profane history, with no intention of verifying the divine claim, does in effect yield evidence that might be so interpreted. Our own times especially do.

We have not yet seen the end of the worst perpetration of atrocities ever known to the world; the slaughtered victims have numbered beyond the reach of an accurate count into the untold millions; the enslavement of large areas of people remains an accepted status quo because no responsible government dares to challenge the injustice out of fear of igniting a global holocaust. In view of this, no student of the times can miss the enormity of the ugly facts. And the infidel who disallows any outside influence in the world's affairs will be hard-pressed to explain the inhuman cruelties.

The facts do not flatter our humanity. Tyrants drunk with power, having beguiled or intimidated nations into carrying out their wicked designs, have had the helpless herded together to be shipped off in boxcars to concentration camps, or stuffed alive into ovens, or thrust into torture chambers to be brainwashed, or into dungeons to go mad. Aldous Huxley has hit upon the perfect name for the scoundrels: "Petty Lucifers." And if these miniatures of Satan are in fact only his ignorant dupes or even his psychopathic puppets, and not his knowing agents, what difference does it make as to the diabolic results? They have all by the merits of their record come quite honestly by the name.

Who knows how much of the strife within nations, or between nations, between the races, is attributable to what St. Paul would call the wiles
of the devil? Wise to the ways of hell, the shrewd
apostle in singling out its worst schemer did not
for a moment doubt that Satan had the cooperation
of all the other hating devils. "We are not con-
tending against flesh and blood, but against . . . the
spiritual hosts of wickedness," he writes to the
Ephesians, seeing through the human antagonisms
to the prime source of the trouble.[1]

No sillier form of escapism is possible to a man
of faith than to dismiss from his consideration the
malice of hell as none of his concern. "Be watchful," St. Peter would advise him. "Your adversary
the devil prowls around like a roaring lion, seeking
someone to devour."[2] And with what infinite pathos
had not the prince of the apostles himself been so
informed! "Simon, Simon," he heard from a voice
not to be doubted, "behold, Satan demanded to have
you, that he might sift you like wheat, but I have
prayed for you that your faith may not fail."[3]

It did not fail. But the faith of another apostle
did. He betrayed the noblest of masters. Nor did
the poor wretch realize he had been tricked into this
lowest form of treachery until he felt the first ter-

---

[1] Eph. 6:12.
[2] 1 Pet. 5:8.
[3] Luke 22:31.

rorizing pangs of despair. Tricked by whom? "The devil," St. John gives answer, "put it into the heart of Judas Iscariot, Simon's son, to betray him."[4]

At the Last Supper, after Judas had gone, Jesus, who knew how roughly the world would treat the apostles, did not pray to his Father to "take them out of the world." His prayer for them had a different purpose. He prayed to his heavenly Father to "keep them from the evil one."[5]

The Lord never underestimates the evil power of Satan. He knows, among other calamities, what a dreadful loss of faith is everywhere due to him. His parables bristle with warnings. "The seed is the word of God," he explains in his story about the sower. "The ones along the path are those who have heard; then the devil comes and takes away the word from their hearts, that they may not believe and be saved."[6]

And St. Paul, writing his advice to Timothy concerning wayward young widows, grieves that "some have already strayed after Satan."[7] The apostle does not hush up an ugly fact: he calls the devil's bluff. "We are not ignorant of his designs," he informs the Corinthians with almost the air of a boast.[8] But he does not minimize the effectiveness of those

---

[4] John 13:2.
[5] *Ibid.* 17:15.
[6] Luke 8:11-12.
[7] 1 Tim. 5:15.
[8] 2 Cor. 2:11.

insidious designs. "The god of this world," he declares of the archfiend, "has blinded the minds of the unbelievers, to keep them from seeing the light of the Gospel."[9]

The subtlety of Satan, the shrewd power of his malice, his pious pretenses, the way he goes about perverting the faithful through human agents who may not themselves realize that they are his stooges: none of this escapes the vigilance of the alert apostle. And he always responds with a contempt for the infernal deceiver second only to his sympathy for the deceived. Learning of an erroneous faction of teachers at work among the Corinthians, and knowing under whose influence the faction worked, whether these false prophets knew it or not, he writes to his imperiled converts in sorrow: "I am afraid that as the serpent deceived Eve by his cunning, your thoughts will be led astray from a sincere and pure devotion to Christ."[10]

The false prophets, who are a danger to souls, are rebuked in genuine charity in the Epistles. Their charismatic claims do not deceive St. Paul. He understands what unholy spirit has prompted their action: and all his warnings to the faithful go beyond these human agents to the evil mastermind. "I appeal to you, brethren, to take note of those who create dissensions and difficulties, in opposition to

---

[9] *Ibid.* 4:4.
[10] *Ibid.* 11:3.

the doctrines which you have been taught; avoid them. For such persons do not serve our Lord Christ, but their own appetites, and by fair and flattering words they deceive the hearts of the simpleminded."[11] Don't worry, Satan has not been overlooked! He bears the brunt of the invective: "I would have you wise as to what is good and guileless as to what is evil; then the God of peace will soon crush Satan under your feet."[12]

Call this craftiest of all deceivers Satan, the devil, the serpent, Beelzebub or Lucifer, he remains by any name the implacable foe who would stop at nothing to pervert the human race. He and his legions of evil spirits simply do not like our kind, bearing us a grudge, meaning by every stratagem in their power to dupe us out of the prospective beatitude they could have had and rejected. Feeling the misery of their loss even while they will it, they are not good losers. They want no lesser creatures to fill their vacancies in heaven. They are furious haters.

The devil of devils has their help in his seduction of the faithful. And St. Paul, in his predilection for Satan as a fit subject for treatment, does by no means neglect the others. He calls attention to them all. "In later times," he predicts for the benefit of a future generation, "some will depart from the faith by giving heed to deceitful spirits and doc-

---

[11] Rom. 16:17-18.
[12] *Ibid.* 16:19-20.

trines of demons, through the pretensions of liars
whose consciences are seared."[13] Now that is strong
language! But St. Paul was himself only heeding,
and in the charity of his apostolic soul would have
others heed with him, the divine cry: "Beware of
false prophets!"

His warnings are in every instance motivated by
charity. The deposit of faith was to him a God-
given treasury of truths to be guarded against spo-
liation: they were his great joy in life, and he would
have all mankind share his happy certitude. "O
Timothy," he ends his letter in a tender admonition
against substituting learned theories for the change-
less creed, "guard what has been entrusted to you.
Avoid the godless chatter and contradictions of what
is falsely called knowledge, for by professing it some
have missed the mark as regards the faith. Grace
be with you."[14]

No one has to tell St. Paul that, to avoid playing
directly into the clutches of Satan, every show of
indignation against apostasy must remain pure of
rancor toward the apostate. He knows that a hate-
ridden soul has already fallen prey to the diabolical
influence and so, realizing the delicacy of balance
to be maintained, he advises: "Be angry but do not
sin; do not let the sun go down on your anger, and

---

[13] 1 Tim. 4:1-2.
[14] *Ibid.* 6:20-21.

give no opportunity to the devil."[15] The idea that sin opens the soul to the devil and that virtue closes him out, recurs regularly in the Epistles. Let us forgive one another our grievances, it is accordingly proposed to the Corinthians, "to keep Satan from gaining the advantage over us."[16]

St. Paul must have been a dreadful frustration to Satan. He was always being kind to people, and never more kind to them than when he strove to break the devil's hold on them. Where could one look to find a more benevolent directive to any responsible custodian of the faith, so considerate of him who must administer the rebuke to his flock, so urgent with hope for the wayward, so wise to the malice of hell, than once again in Paul's guidelines to his beloved co-worker Timothy? "The Lord's servant," he writes, "must not be quarrelsome but kindly to every one, an apt teacher, forbearing, correcting his opponents with gentleness. God may perhaps grant that they will repent and come to know the truth, and they may escape from the snare of the devil, after being captured by him to do his will."[17]

Satan and his evil spirits can and sometimes do assume physical form to further their sinister designs. They are reported to have done so, in Scrip-

---

[15] Eph. 4:26-27.
[16] 2 Cor. 2:11.
[17] 2 Tim. 2:24-26.

ture, and in hagiography. They can inflict bodily
as well as spiritual harm: the evangelist Luke cites
an instance in which Satan had crippled a woman
for eighteen years; Jesus cured the woman in a moment.[18] Our haters from hell have also entered
human bodies to torment them, to use them vilely:
demoniac possession stands out as an indisputable
fact of the Gospels.[19] And in profane accounts the
chronicler has no explanation to offer, who rejects
the religious one.

The evil spirits, banished from heaven, have not
been confined to hell in the sense that they cannot
by dint of their great natural agility intrude upon
our world. For this reason some theologians prefer
to call hell a state of being rather than a locale.
Diabolical influence will not be totally crushed until
doomsday, when the whole human race from Adam
to the final generation will stand divided between
the blessed, forever secure from hell, and the
damned, forever its captives. The conflict will then
have reached a permanent conclusion.

The fallen angels, who would hate us into hell
if given the opportunity, cannot tolerate the faith
which would guide us to heaven. It infuriates them.
It cannot but enrage them with its great truth: that
the holy angels of God who are their conquerors
from an ancient war are ever available to us. We

---

[18] See Luke 13:10-16.

[19] See Matt. 10:1; Mark 3:15; Luke 8:1-3.

may have their protective intimacy for the asking. "Are they not all ministering spirits sent forth to serve, for the sake of those who are to obtain salvation?"[20]

And what draws them to us, as it repels the forces of evil, is the virtue that includes all virtues. Charity, the love of God and neighbor, is the mighty resistant to hell. Satan, the father of hatred, and the lesser devils with him, cannot withstand it. And the angels of love cannot but gather around a soul imbued with it. "Do not neglect to show hospitality to strangers," is an inspired piece of advice, "for thereby some have entertained angels unawares."[21]

---

[20] Heb. 1:14.
[21] *Ibid.* 13:2.

What the Angels Do

THE ANGELS did not have to be told by the three young men in the fiery furnace to praise the Lord.[1] They were already doing it. They still are. And their devotion never tires. To honor their gracious God, adore him, express to him their love: this is their primary function, their supreme delight.

They remain ever at his service. The prophet Daniel, with no pretense at a correct estimate of the angelic multitude crowding his vision, reports with wild abandon that "a thousand thousand served him, and ten thousand times ten thousand stood before him."[2] In his similar vision of their praising God, the apostle John heard what must have been to human ear a torrential melody: "the voice of many angels, numbering myriads of myriads and thousands of thousands."[3] Nor did the Psalmist, knowing his angels, exclude a single one of them from his invitation: "Bless the Lord, O you his angels, you mighty ones who do his word, hearkening to the voice of his word!"[4]

---

[1] See Dan. 3:37.

[2] *Ibid.* 7:10.

[3] Rev. 5:11.

[4] Ps. 103 (102):20.

To obey his sovereign will, adore his infinite holiness, ever rejoice to a point of ecstasy in his presence, are all one with the angels. A continuous refrain of "Holy, holy, holy," is what Isaiah heard the seraphim chant as he watched their acts of worship.[5] No vision to the prophets has ever shown a single member of the heavenly choirs grown indifferent to their jubilee. They never tire of singing out their joy to the Most High.

No vision of the celestial choirs can include any but a segment — as art does — of heaven's many angels. It can only suggest, as art does, their innumerability. Who has not looked up into the dome of some great basilica to admire a workmanship that could so paint or sculpture a ceiling as to suggest an opening in the sky and in that opening a tumbling sea of angels? None of us would think of counting, nor are we supposed to think of counting, such a wild density of cherubs alive with adoration. We nevertheless get the idea.

Another thing the angels do, while forever praising God, is reflect his glory. Created more closely in his image, they do it better than man does. St. Joan used to marvel at the splendor of her angelic visions. But what she saw did not reveal to the girl anything near St. Michael's true magnificence.

Visionaries have had all they could do, finding on earth nothing worth a comparison, to describe

[5] Isa. 6:3.

the splendor of their angelic visions as well as they did. Dante, realizing this, does not try a direct, but resorts to an indirect, description of the angel who approaches him in the *Purgatorio:*

> . . . more bright
> Appeared the bird of God, nor could the eye
> Endure his splendor near: I mine bent down.

Thus it was with Anna Catherine Emmerich, whose frequent apparitions of her guardian angel admitted of a free and easy conversation between them but not a steady gaze from her. It would have blinded her. Able always to notice his resplendent human form and luminous robes, however, the favored mystic confided to her amanuensis, "I can never look him full in the face."

To reflect the glory of God while praising and obeying and loving him remains to the angels their common activity. However, since Scripture itself divides the angels into nine ranks, an attempt has been made to assign to each of the nine a special function within the general scheme. The standard book of reference on the subject carries the title *De coelesti hierarchia.* Originally ascribed to Dionysius the Areopagite, it has since been credited to an anonymous writer of the early sixth century. Whoever he may be, the author arranges his classification into three hierarchies in their order of importance:

Seraphim, Cherubim, Thrones
Dominations, Virtues, Powers
Principalities, Archangels, Angels.

If the last-mentioned of the choirs has been given the name of "angels," the word is far more often used generically to mean any angel, regardless of rank. Every seraph is an angel. So is every cherub. An angel is an angel no matter in what choir he sings. But if he belongs to the lowest, he is in a double sense an angel.

That the dictionary allows this double use of the word "angel" is attributable to *De coelesti hierarchia.* The treatise has exerted an undoubted influence. One needn't probe deeply into the later patristic writings to find its arguments widely accepted there. St. Ambrose, St. Gregory the Great, St. John Damascene, and others of their privileged circle, though by no means all, agree with them.

St. Augustine, one of the greatest, does not. He accepts the ninefold division of angels on the authority of Holy Scripture. But when it comes to discerning in detail the gradational arrangement as put forth in the book, he finds the distinctions too badly blurred to be of any use. Citing St. Paul's discriminative run of words, "whether thrones or dominations or principalities or powers,"[6] he raises an honest question. "What difference of rank do these

---

[6] Col. 1:16 (according to the Vulgate).

four terms connote?" And he promptly replies: "Let those say who can. As for me, I confess I haven't the slightest idea."

To a sharp mind, such as his, the book cannot but prove disappointing. Its classifications are not clear-cut. They overlap. They get jumbled together.

The seraphim are accorded the highest rank because, on the word of the prophet, they unceasingly chant their praises to the Most Holy. But does not the Bible have all the angels in heaven doing that? Wherein lies the distinction? How does the common practice distinguish the seraphim from the rest? It would have to be a question on their part of stronger intensity; and this, of course, could be the case; their very name means "to be on fire, to be ardent." But Scripture only implies it, at most.

Does not Pseudo-Dionysius himself speak of the angels in general as the celestial choirs? He exempts none from the divine praises. Nor does the liturgy. The new order of the Mass, while dropping from its Prefaces the names of the various choirs, still has them doing what they have always done. "Countless hosts of angels," goes an invocation to the Most High, "stand before you to do your will; they look upon your splendor and praise you, night and day." And again, "all the choirs of angels" join in this unending hymn.

The breviary by its very enumeration of them admits the gradational choirs. But St. Augustine admits them, too, as he would admit the division of mankind into races. His lone contention is that the cited scriptural evidence is not sufficiently sharp to convey any but a vague understanding of the distinctions at best, and with reference to the thrones and dominations and principalities and powers, no understanding at all.

Yet, what of that? All nine choirs, each according to its capacity, serve a single unity of purpose. Every angel of the lowest order has a voice in the action, and were his voice lacking, the loss would by just so much weaken the total harmony. Heaven would miss it. A philharmonic conductor does not belittle the gentle efforts of the flute, nor does he ask whether the trumpets or violins, or whichever of the assorted instruments, contribute most to the symphony when it is the combination of their differences that so completely entrances.

"We say," writes Pope St. Gregory, "that there exist nine orders of angels because we know it from Scripture to be true." He admiringly accepts the information, seeing in it new evidence of an almighty resourcefulness. Yet still more does he admire, as a richer indication of this, the far greater variety by which each angel of heaven differs from every other, though their multitudes from scriptural accounts would seem to outnumber the stars. When our Lord said that, if he asked for them, his Father would send him "more than twelve legions of angels,"[7] it was tantamount to saying, in view of the numerical size of a military legion at the time, more than 72,000. It was again a reference to the vast innumerability of the angels: the wonder of which sharpens the additional wonder that of so countless a total not a single one but enjoys within his choir and indeed within all heaven an individuality that makes him a unique species of his own.

We see the same diverse law of identity at work in the animal world: and who of us, reflecting, can fail to feel with St. Gregory the wonder of it? A monkey looks just enough like a man to excite our mirth, but not enough to confuse us into thinking them of the same species. We never see the man locked into the monkey's cage by mistake. The two are distinguishable.

But so are twin sisters. Identical twins do not exist. The term is a misnomer. Their close resemblance destroys the identity of neither. Only a stranger or casual acquaintance can fail to tell them apart. Their parents never mistake them.

Even when these twins lay in their hospital cribs, shortly after birth, their unique footprints certified their identity. Joan never was, never can be the girl her sister is. She remains nobody but herself. God has not made two of her: one he apparently thought would suffice. Crooned into her youthful ear, the

---

[7] Matt. 26:53.

song would only be telling Joan the truth: "There'll never be another you, dear."

So it is with the angels: only more so. Joan and her sister Jane, for all their separate identity, do belong to the same species, whereas no two angels ever do. Of their trillions upon trillions, every one of them within their common angelhood constitutes a species of his own. The *Summa* elaborates on this, rather unnecessarily, since the elementary difference between any animal and a pure spirit already suggests the reason why. The calf born of a cow, the lamb of a sheep, the baby of a mother, all inherit traits and indeed their very bodies. Every kitten with its tiny whiskers implies the many whiskered cats that have formed its pedigree. Every boy with eyes in his head got them, through a long lineage of ancestors, from Adam and Eve. The angel, on the contrary, inherits nothing of other angels; he has not come of other angels; direct from God, his individuality owes not a thing to them. It is more sharply his than Joan's weaker identification distinguishes her. No twins are to be found among the angelic choirs.

The prodigious variety among the angels within their respective choirs, and the dissimilarities between choir and choir, exceed the norms of human comparison. The variations in the material world between star and star, animal and animal, or whatever else, cannot compare. To study the faces of a multitude and take notice that no two are precisely alike, though all sufficiently alike to retain the identity of faces: this is to receive no adequate idea of that stronger versatility which has called into being the countless angels and, without rescinding their common characteristics, has given to each an individuality unmatched in creation. Every angel reflects in a manner unique to himself something of his Creator's infinite beauty.

And this giving glory to God, on the part of every angel, by his mirroring forth some distinct facet of the Omnipotent Grandeur, though it may escape human recognition, does not go unappreciated. Their Creator knows what the angels are thus doing. It is not an idle display. They are themselves appreciative of their strong singularity, praising their Maker for it. It is not wasted.

Because of the angels, nothing created is wasted. We must not therefore think of them, whose home is heaven, as outsiders to our world. They relate to it. They enrich it. They complete its meaning.

Were it not for them, who of God's intelligent creatures could appreciate as a display of his glory any but an infinitesimal part of the universe? How little of its complicated mysteries, its magnitude, does the human mind comprehend! The universe withholds from us many times more secrets than science has learned. But the angels, understanding the immensity and variety and harmony of it, see there in full what we can see only in part, the handiwork of the Omnipotent.

Their involvement in the universe takes on another activity. It includes their custody of mankind. It is another of their services to Providence, whose will is theirs. What God desires of them, that the angels do. It is what they also desire. "In la sua volontade è nostra pace," sang the poet who knows them best. His words sum up the essence of their beatitude.

IX

Three Stand Out by Name

THE ANGELS, without interrupting their adoration, attend to God's interests on earth. "I am Raphael, one of the seven holy angels who present the prayers of the saints," the angel at his side told Tobias, finally disclosing his identity, and implying that, while he had been walking the earth an apparent youth, he was no absentee from heaven.[1] By his own admission, he enjoyed with six others a special place of honor there.

The seven would seem, from a composite of scriptural texts, to have been so closely taken into God's confidence that our petitions to the Holy One are their immediate concern. They certainly were to Raphael. "When you and your daughter-in-law Sarah prayed," he informed the grateful old father of Tobias, "I brought a reminder of your prayer before the Holy One."[2]

The angel went on to say, lest he be given undue credit, that his mission on earth to befriend young Tobias, arrange for his wedding with Sarah, break the devil's power over their marriage, and restore sight to the old father, was not originally his idea

[1] Tob. 12:15.

[2] *Ibid.* 12:12.

at all. Glad to have been of such help, this angel of the most endearing courtesy didn't think the thanks should go to him. Let the praise go where it belongs: "I did not come as a favor on my part, but by the will of God. Therefore praise him for ever."[3]

It is one of the kindlier mysteries of life that the angels, while tending to their divine business in heaven, are not unaware of us. The wonder of this does not discredit it. Does the skeptic doubt that a pilot flying his ship over the Alleghenies can without taking his mind from the controls think of his infant daughter back home in Santa Barbara? Her guardian angel, no less devotedly, watches over the child while he continues to share with the rest of heaven its uninterruptible bliss.

What was it that Raphael, with his ready charm, said to Tobit upon his return to the old gentleman after an absence of weeks? "When you buried the dead," a fact nobody had told the angel, "I was likewise present with you. When you did not hesitate to rise and leave your dinner in order to lay out the dead, your good deed was not hidden from me, but I was with you."[4] In other words, his embodiment as a youth did not deprive him of his angelic agility. It did not confine his spirit. Accompanying Tobias, he was at the same time aware of

[3] *Ibid.* 12:18.
[4] *Ibid.* 12:12-13.

the old father at home. His benignity knew no bounds.

The archangel, along with Michael and Gabriel, has his new feast on September 29. He is invoked as the patron of travelers, since he went with Tobias on a long journey from Nineveh to a city of the Medes; as a healer of the sick, since he cured a grateful old man of his blindness; as the promoter of happy marriages, since he found a perfect bride for Tobias; as a deliverer from evil, since he freed young Sarah of a devil; as a member, finally, of that special inner cordon of seven before the Most Holy. No other angel is so variously invoked.

Of his prerogatives, his power to heal receives perhaps the emphasis. His very name means "God has healed." But the Vesper hymn for his former feast puts as much stress on his power to guide. "Descend from heaven, O Raphael, Angel-Physician," it pleads, "to heal our ills, to guide our erring steps."

Another of the angels who with Raphael belongs to the special group of seven, and one of the three to be mentioned in Scripture by name, is Gabriel.[5] When one evening Daniel prayed to heaven, an angelic apparition quickly responded. It was Gabriel in human form. The prophet himself has so described him. "While I was praying, the man Ga-

---

[5] Luke 1:19.

briel, whom I had seen in the vision from the first, came to me in swift flight."[6]

It was not the last time they would meet face to face. They did so again, as recorded a page later. This time the angel's face shone like a flash of lightning, his stature was that of a robust giant, and his voice sounded "like the noise of a multitude." Overawed, the prophet swooned. He couldn't stop himself. "No strength was left in me," he explains.[7]

Not that Daniel was to be pitied! As before, the angel had come in answer to a prayer. Shaking the prophet awake, the angel bade him not to fear, "for from the first day that you set your mind to understand and humbled yourself before God, your words have been heard, and I have come because of your words."[8] How often in Scripture has not St. Gabriel come to his visionaries while they were at prayer!

Whenever in sacred eloquence there occurs the expression Angel of the Incarnation, it refers to Gabriel. In use from the earliest days of the Church, it remains a favorite epithet. It deserves to be. The angel has earned it.

He it was who predicted to Daniel the time of the Messiah's birth. He announced to Zechariah in the Sanctuary the birth of the precursor, John the Baptist. He brought to Mary direct from heaven

---

[6] Dan. 9:21.

[7] *Ibid.* 10:6-9.

[8] *Ibid.* 10:12.

the invitation to become the mother of the Son of
God, an honor that would raise her to a dignity
above that of the angels themselves.[9] No queen
ever received from an envoy the courtesy shown
here. The angel who had overpowered the prophet
stood himself in awe of Mary.

He may have appeared, and according to a pious
but not extravagant opinion did appear, to others
than Mary, Zechariah and Daniel.

An angel, radiant with glory, proclaimed from
the skies the birth of "a Savior, who is Christ the
Lord." An angel, in advance of the sacred birth,
had counseled a worried Joseph; an angel, after the
birth, warned him to flee into Egypt with Child and
Mother; an angel, when the danger had passed, once
more appeared to the foster father to let him know
that the return to Israel would now be safe.[10] Clearly,
heaven was looking after the Holy Family.

Nor did this solicitude end with the infancy of
Christ. It was still in evidence on the eve of his
death. In the Garden of Gethsemane while Jesus
prayed in great anguish of spirit "there appeared
to him an angel from heaven, strengthening him."[11]
Even from his tomb, when by his own power he arose

---

[9] See *ibid.* 9:25-26; Luke 1:19; 1:26.
[10] Luke 2:10-11; Matt. 1:20; 2:13; 2:19.
[11] Luke 22:43.

as from a siesta, an accommodating angel rolled back the stone.[12]

Was this unnamed angel always a different one? Or was he in all six instances one and the same? Since in the apparitions on behalf of the Incarnate Savior the angel has been identified several times as Gabriel, tradition is inclined to believe it was also he on the occasions the angel has gone unnamed. It might well be. In her account of her vision of the Agony in the Garden, Sister Emmerich does not hesitate to identify the comforting angel as Gabriel.

This great angel has acquired for himself a new honor. He has of late years been chosen the patron of the Catholic Broadcasters' Association, which confers annually its *Gabriels* on radio and TV producers for quality programs. These golden statuettes stand on not a few mantels in American homes as a direct tribute to their winners and as an indirect tribute to the angel whose broadcast from the skies broke the news of the most blessed of blessed events to the world. His words had a long way to go. But the angel got them down with ease to the shepherds without benefit of microphone. His voice had power.

He is, by the very definition of his name, the angel of strength. The liturgy so refers to him. It is his sobriquet in an ancient liturgical chant still

---

[12] See Matt. 28:2.

in use, "Christ, Glory of the Holy Angels." The hymn, invoking by name the aid of Gabriel and Michael and Raphael, leaves out none of the unnamed others. It calls upon them all.

And that suggests an important conclusion. It is not necessary that angels belong to a certain choir or to a special group within the choir to heed our prayers. Their whole company without exception find it an essential of their beatitude to help those whom the God of their love wants them to help. Nobody's guardian angel ever falls asleep. Heaven remains awake, heedful of our sincere pleas.

Scripture has told us enough of the angels, and how they minister to our world, to inculcate a profound respect for them. From what it has related in detail of a comparative few, we learn to understand the many others. No believer in his right mind would slight any of the angels. No believer with any sense could fail to respond to the benevolence of Raphael, the high demeanor of Gabriel. Neither would the sane of faith neglect a third, whom Scripture names with lavish praise.

We have no exhaustive *Who's Who* from eternity to consult. But we do have the Bible, and from it many expositors have drawn sufficient evidence to rate Michael the greatest angel in heaven. It could be. It would prove worth looking into. His importance urges the attempt.

X

The Prince of Angels

IF ACTION SPEAKS LOUDER than words; if what a person does reveals his true evaluation better than what is merely said of him; then Michael may well hold, as his champions say he does, first place among the angels. He it was who showed the boldest reaction to the threat upon the majesty of God and, of all the heavenly host, rushed to the forefront in the fight against Satan. He led. He confronted Satan directly. Does he not therefore deserve a commensurate reward? Did he not thereby gain the primacy among angels?

The affirmative reply which the question expects does not enjoy airtight certitude. The appraisal may be, has been, opposed by counter-considerations. The argument must rely, as must its attempted refutation, on whatever evidence Scripture affords: and Scripture, while it has dropped suggestions, has issued no direct statement either way. The Bible, in fact, has restricted its more definite information about the angels to a few; nor does it go into unnecessary detail about these. It tells us no more than we need to know.

What, then, could have induced a set of self-appointed judges to choose one from the angelic multitudes and with confidence declare him the greatest? These advocates obviously liked the quality of the implicit evidence. From it, in no uncertain terms, they drew their conclusion. They had no doubt of its validity. They defended it.

But are they right?

How could the judges of a world-wide beauty contest, if a profane parallel may be admitted, go home certain they had picked the absolute paragon of women? They selected their Miss Universe from no very large range of candidates but from a survival of the few, none of whom had had to stand competition from the unknown majority of beauties who were not entered in the local preliminaries at all.

The parallel does not pretend to be exact. Admittedly, such a contest involves only a fraction of the eligible population: whereas, according to St. Michael's advocates, Scripture includes all the holy angels, leaving out none, when it names him their leader against the forces of Satan. This carries weight. It is not easily minimized.

The text reads, it will be recalled: "Now war arose in heaven, Michael and his angels fighting against the dragon: and the dragon and his angels fought, but they were defeated."[1] There, as surely as Satan has been designated the archdevil, Michael is taken for granted as the foremost angel of heaven. So contend his champions, who do not restrict the

---

[1] Rev. 12:7-8.

phrase "Michael and his angels" to mean "Michael and his particular choir of angels." They heartily agree with the liturgy, which they helped to form, that he is without reservation *the Prince of the Heavenly Hosts.*

St. Basil, and the Greek Fathers almost to the man, and such luminaries of the Western Church as St. Robert Bellarmine, to name one of the more insistent among them, have found the scriptural evidence sufficient to establish the outright supremacy of Michael. They make light of the counterargument that he belongs to one of the lower ranks. They accordingly interpret the Biblical title "Michael the Archangel"[2] to mean "Michael the most eminent of the angels." They do not think that Scripture intends us to believe that Michael is just another of the archangels, a heavenly choir which ranks eighth, and next to lowest, of the angelic choirs. Else, the argument goes, why does Scripture apply the title *archangel* to Michael alone? Neither Raphael nor Gabriel is anywhere in the Bible so called. A unique title, signifying his preeminence, it is in that sense reserved to Michael.

Others follow a little different twist to the argument. Equally intent on ensuring Michael his primacy, they associate him with the highest of the nine choirs, the seraphim, according him the highest place among them. And that, as if to take no

[2] Jude 1:9.

chances, is designed to make assurance doubly sure. It definitely, determinedly, and almost to the point of cheerful defiance, puts Michael at the top.

Most of his advocates, however, while admitting the nine gradational ranks of angels, deem it unnecessary to identify Michael with the seraphim in order to ensure his supremacy. They see no discrepancy between acknowledging his lower natural rank, if so it was, and at the same time favoring his ascendancy over the whole realm of angels by virtue of his stronger response to grace than theirs. Remember that hierarchy among the angels is not a question of grace but of nature. It was already established at the time (as St. Paul makes clear) when an unnamed percentage of the principalities and the powers fell from heaven.[3] It arranges its subjects into ranks according to their created nature; so that once an archangel, to take an example, always an archangel; although by the grace of God and his cooperation with it an archangel could rise above his nature to transcend even the seraphim.

Keep in mind, the angels once underwent a test; their wills had been free to take or leave the Beatific Vision; their wills had even been free to decide the degree of their devotion to the Most High. And so, with the reward proportionate to his use of grace, there is no reason why a particular angel could not have been promoted to a supremacy over others

---

[3] See Eph. 6:12.

who had once excelled him. Justly appreciative, God has the power to show his appreciation.

The Mother of God's own Son, by her human nature an inferior creature to the angels, is now in her glorification their Queen. The Creator can exalt the worthy to a dignity beyond their natural status. Do we not see on earth an occasional person of no outstanding natural endowment become a saint to be looked up to? He shows forth a superiority which his intellectual or physical betters cannot match.

St. Michael has been classified a seraph, an archangel (in the hierarchical sense) and even a member of the lowest order, though its principal one. The authorities cannot make up their minds, to any degree of conformity, in what choir to place the prince of angels. But what does he care, knowing himself how he stands with God, where they rank him?

His boosters, to sum up their argument, are not concerned that other angels may have been created his superiors. Let him belong to whatever choir, to the lowest, or to that of the archangels, as is commonly believed — he still could have received top honors. He would remain by nature an archangel, if archangel he had been created, but by his superlative response to grace would have been elevated to the primacy. Does not the glorified Mother of

Christ, retaining her womanhood, now transcend the angels?

Tradition, with certain correlative passages from the Old Testament to rely on, associates Michael with Gabriel and Raphael as of the privileged seven who wait upon the Throne of the Almighty and carry his more important messages to mankind. Who, incidentally, might the remaining four be? They go unnamed in the Canonical Books. But writers of the apocrypha, whose effort is frowned upon, have supplied the additional names of the septet: Uriel, Raguel, Sariel, Jeremiel.

Of all the angels, Michael was the prime favorite of Israel. The Chosen People acknowledged him as their patron, their protector, their guardian. It was not wishful dreaming. They had the assurance of Holy Writ. "Michael, the great prince, who has charge of your people," another angel so describes him to the prophet Daniel.[4]

In the Pentateuch and the Historical Books of the Old Testament there recurrently appears "the angel of the Lord" or "the angel of God," who sometimes speaks as though he were the Lord God himself. In Exodus he is even so called: "And the Lord went before them by day in a pillar of cloud to lead them along the way, and by night in a pillar of fire to give them light, that they might travel by day and

---

[4] Dan. 12:1.

by night."[5] But then this heavenly guide, who is there called the Lord, shortly becomes again "the angel of God."[6] From this St. Jerome, with a large following that includes St. Augustine, has concluded that he is an angel indeed, yet so commissioned to act in the Lord's name and vested with such authority that he speaks as though he were the Lord. "Give heed to him," the Lord himself advises Moses; "... for my name is in him."[7]

So majestic, so highly privileged an angel—would he be Michael? None other, insist the majority of the traditional commentators.

Christendom equally claims St. Michael for its special champion against evil. Leaf through the standard hymnals still widely in use, and it will be seen from the lyrics in his honor that his guardianship is taken for granted. The prince of the heavenly hosts is constantly, in some such wording, being implored to put the prince of devils in his place. The Bible has surely served notice that "at that time," meaning the end of the world, when antichrist shall have come, "shall arise Michael, the great prince,"[8] to confine the onslaught of evil once and for all to hell.

---

[5] Ex. 13:21.

[6] *Ibid.* 14:19.

[7] *Ibid.* 23:21.

[8] Dan. 12:1.

The Anglican Book of Common Prayer reserves a date in September for the feast of *St. Michael and All Angels,* and if that does not suggest Michael's primacy what then do the words connote? He alone of the angels receives mention, and twice at that, in the old Confiteor, still in use at Compline. He alone of the angels, at the Requiem Mass, is asked to conduct "the souls of all the faithful departed into the holy light." It is again his name that gets into the liturgical prayer for the dying, a farewell of what tender confidence: "Receive your servant, O Lord, into your kingdom. May he (or she) be taken up by holy Michael, the archangel of God."

Such consistent partiality cannot but establish Michael the favorite angel of the liturgy. It does more. It gives support to the widespread belief in his priority in heaven, his absolute supremacy among the celestial choirs.

The Fathers of the Church, custodians of the faith in their day, were inclined to think that the angel who blocked the way of Balaam, and the angel who destroyed Sennacherib's army before it could destroy Jerusalem, and the angel who appeared on the scene time and again to avert disaster from the Israelites, was in every instance their guardian angel.[9] Nor has Michael denied his availability to the later needs of the faithful. We do not know

---

[9] See Num. 22:22; 2 Kings (4 Kings) 19:35.

how often, when the future foreboded unusual evil, the great warrior of God intervened through his apparitions to this or that saint of the hour to swing the turn of events. After all, these visionaries whom he guided would only disclose their experience when practically forced to it. But we have from them enough reports to confirm Michael's reputation.

Satan, the father of hatred, and his legions of secondary devils, lack omnipotence. Their malice cannot touch the Almighty. Nor can they withstand his loyal angels, whose love is stronger than the hatred of the fallen angels. Michael, the prince of the heavenly hosts, proved himself too much for Satan.

Was it Michael whom Our Lady of Guadalupe portrayed, beneath her own representation, in the only known painting by a resident of heaven? Or, in deference to a girlhood acquaintance, was it Gabriel? It may have been either. It may have been neither. The artist hasn't said. Whatever the identity, their Queen did all the angels a favor in depicting one of them in fadeless pigments on a flimsy *tilma*. She was asserting to the world, to the millions of eyes that would view the painting, her absolute belief in the reality of his glorious kind.

Guardian Angels

IF ST. MICHAEL has been called the angel of Israel, and so called by a fellow angel at that, Scripture does not let the matter rest there. It implies that other nations enjoy the custody of a special angel, too. It openly states that the Persians do, and the Greeks: then, inferentially, why not the others?[1]

"Why not indeed!" would express the unwavering reaction of the Fathers. They didn't argue the point. They accepted the inference as a logical consequent. Their consensus has established a tradition.

It also invites a question. If every nation has an angel to watch out for it, why should the world have got into its present mess? For the same obvious reason that an individual, who has his own private angel, can make a mess of life. How the nation feels toward virtue, whether its people respect or contemn it, and to what degree, determines the amount of aid to be received. Heaven doesn't force its favors; the proper disposition is what attracts them. Yet, for as long as the nation survives, on account of the good that may lurk in the wayward

---

[1] See Dan. 10:13, 20.

populace, the good that may come of its gropings, its angel is there to render service.

In the clearest of words the Lord assured the Israelites of strong protection: "Behold, I send an angel before you, to guard you on the way and to bring you to the place which I have prepared."[2] And the angel did. He made good the Lord's promise. He guided the people through every besetting danger to their destined land. No police escort could have done so well, could have done it at all.

But, if the nation as a unit lies open to threats, what about the individual? Sharing with others a common guardian, a person could use an angel of his own. God does not stint his aid. Every man, woman and child, thanks to Providence, has such an angel.

Jacob acknowledged his indebtedness to "the angel who has redeemed me from all evil."[3] Abraham, for another, endorsed the cult of the angel guardian. His was a confidence that does not question. Dispatching his steward on an important mission, the patriarch reassured him that "the Lord, the God of heaven, . . . will send his angel before you."[4]

An angel appeared to Hagar when she went wandering into the desert, and sent her safely back

---

[2] Ex. 23:20.

[3] Gen. 48:16.

[4] *Ibid.* 24:7.

to her mistress.[5] An angel announced to Manoah's discouraged wife, who was barren, that she would bear a son; and she did; she called him Samson.[6] An angel directed Gideon to turn the tide of events from a seven-year enslavement to a great national rescue.[7] If the angel on any of these occasions did not happen to be the people's, it is safe to conclude that he was the individual's.

The angel who fed Elijah in the desert acted as his guardian. Feeling desperately alone, hungry, weary of life, the prophet had fallen asleep in the shade of a juniper tree, only to be awakened to a long-needed breakfast. "Arise and eat," said the angel, referring to a miraculous cake that was suddenly there. Had the angel himself made it? No earthly chef could have. The prophet, we are told, "went in the strength of that food forty days and forty nights to Horeb, the mount of God."[8]

The many references to the guardianship of angels in the Old Testament find their confirmation in the New Testament. Our Lord himself gave the doctrine its final sanction. When the devil quoted to him the Psalms about the protective solicitude of angels — "lest you strike your foot against a

---

[5] See *ibid.* 16:7-9.

[6] See Judg. 13:3.

[7] See *ibid.* 6:11ff.

[8] 1 Kings (3 Kings) 19:4-8.

stone" — Jesus implicitly acknowledged the truth of it.[9]

Speaking of the innocence of children, Jesus mentions endearingly in the same breath "their angels."[10] And this prompted St. Jerome to draw a confident conclusion. "So valuable to heaven is the dignity of the human soul," he writes, "that every member of the human race has a guardian angel from the moment the person is born."

But the great Biblicist warns, while he is about it, that what drives their angel from a man or woman is unrepented sin. Neither he nor the rest of the Fathers subscribed to the modern penchant for talking softly or not at all about guilt for fear that it might hurt feelings. They rather thought it was an act of charity toward the guilty to arouse qualms in them. None of them minced his words. "Sin," St. Basil asserts, "turns away angels as smoke turns away bees and a nasty stench puts to flight doves."

In the early years of the Church when persecutions raged, and heavenly intervention was needed most, an angel of the Lord was always there to provide it. He always goes unnamed. Was he, in every instance, the same angel? Could he have been Michael, guardian of the faith? Whoever he was, no opposition could thwart his will.

---

9 Matt. 4:6-7.
10 *Ibid.* 18:10.

Forbidden by the Sanhedrin to preach the doctrines of Christ in the Temple, the apostles nevertheless did, and for the effort got sent to jail. Locking them in did no good.

"At night an angel of the Lord opened the prison doors and brought them out."[11] When the authorities in the morning ordered the captives to be haled before them, the messengers had to return with the report: "We found the prison securely locked and the sentries standing at the doors, but when we opened it we found no one inside."

It is a terribly frustrating experience to fight an angel. But the search continued. Where could the fugitives be? The Sanhedrin had never thought to look near at hand — right under their noses. Yet, near at hand the apostles were; they had been there already from daybreak: back in the Temple making new converts as if they had not been interrupted. The furor that had them surrounded did not bother to close in — until an unofficial busybody tipped off "the officer of the Temple" as to their whereabouts. The account bubbles with mirth.

Other episodes from The Acts of the Apostles which give evidence of how much the angels care, are alive with the same easy mirth. St. Luke must have made a highly desirable conversationalist. In relating another jailbreak, involving a pope and again an angel, he is at his best.

---

[11] Acts 5:19-25.

Herod Agrippa, who then ruled Judea, had already put to death the apostle James, brother of John, and in his persecution of the Christians now ordered Peter's arrest. He went after the big catch. And to make sure his chief prisoner would not escape, the king committed him not only to a cell but to a military guard, four squads of four men each, sixteen soldiers against a rather meek individual. But the odds were not at all in favor of Herod. Peter had the whole Church praying for him.

It was all that was needed. During the night, asleep between two soldiers, his hands fastened by chains, the prison exits guarded by sentries, Peter awakened to a blaze of light in his cell. "Behold, an angel of the Lord appeared," runs the narrative. Get yourself quickly dressed, Peter was told, and suddenly he found he could do this, for "the chains fell off his hands." "Wrap your mantle around you and follow me," said the angel. And Peter did.

The two slipped by the guards and were approaching the iron gate that leads into the city when "it opened to them of its own accord." Only now, two thousand years later, has science caught up with that angelic achievement of forcing a gate to fling itself open to the advance of oncoming pedestrians.

Sensational? Peter thought so. So much so, that it had him wondering for a while whether he might be acting in a dream. It was indeed no dream. No sooner had the two reached the safety of the street than the angel vanished; and the apostle, left to himself, looked about his environment to realize beyond a doubt the reality of his escape. "Now I am sure," he reflected, "that the Lord has sent his angel and rescued me from the hand of Herod."

Peter then headed straight for "the house of Mary, the mother of John whose other name was Mark, where many were gathered together and were praying." The man for whom they prayed, their supreme pontiff, was now knocking at the outer gate. The maid Rhoda ran to open it but, before she did, ran back into the house. "Recognizing Peter's voice," goes the explanation, "in her joy she did not open the gate but ran in and told that Peter was standing at the gate." It couldn't possibly be, was the general reaction to her announcement. "You are mad," Rhoda was told to her face. But she insisted. Then they concluded, as an alternative: "It is his angel!"

Peter, still closed out, could not but have felt a twinge of frustration. Why in heaven's name hadn't the girl unlocked the gate? "Peter continued knocking," wryly remarks the narrator, "and when they opened, they saw him and were amazed." Seeing him, they knew in their astonishment it was not his guardian angel. But at least they had expressed their conviction that the Pope himself had one.[12]

So have we all. The early makers of Christian Tradition were almost unanimous in so thinking.

---

[12] *Ibid.* 12:1-16.

The few dissenters among them, while certainly believing in guardian angels, would restrict the privilege to the faithful, denying it to the infidel. The overwhelming majority allowed no such distinction.

"Every human soul is committed to an angel," writes St. Anselm in accord with the common opinion, but then adds, "when it is united with the body." And there he departs from the general notion that not until birth does the child obtain an angel. Most of the authorities would seem to imply, with St. Jerome, that in sharing the mother's life the unborn child shares the protection of her angel and does not for the time need one of its own. But these are incidental differences.

What matters is that we each have an angel, whenever it was he came into our life, who loves to be with us and even in our disgusting lapses from grace does not lose interest. More than we realize, it is our angel who prompts in us those surprising impulses of good, flashes of enlightenment, surges of confidence, which we credit to our initiative. What sinner has not felt twinges of remorse which he attributes to sheer weariness of experience when an attendant angel may have suggested them? How much of their so-called common sense, which the common people have time and again exerted over a nation to save it from a crisis, is traceable (could we but know) to the nation's guardian angel?

St. Francis de Sales, pausing momentarily in the pulpit before he began his sermons, would always pray to the guardian angels of all the congregation to soften their hearts to his words. He knew where to obtain aid. So did St. Peter Faber. This pious companion of St. Ignatius never entered a town without evoking its guardian angel to help him say the right things to the people.

An angel's influence nonetheless leaves the will free to resist. It does not coerce. It only aids.

Other than moral aid, since our duality includes a body, do the angels supply. St. Paul knew it was his own guardian — "an angel of God to whom I belong" — that would bring him and his fellow passengers all safely to shore when their battered ship would founder. How did he know? The angel had put in an appearance on deck to promise the apostle that. And so it turned out. Not a life was lost, only the ship.[13]

A child, to take another and not unfamiliar example, tumbles from a third-story window to a cement pavement, with nothing apparently to break the fall, and yet escapes injury. Not a bruise does the youngster show, no concussion results. Could it be that the child's angel softened the fall to so harmless an experience? The saints have thought so.

But why, if he can, does not an angel always ward off physical harm to an innocent person under his

---

13 See *ibid*. 27:23-44.

care? For an ulterior good which escapes our notice. A fatal mishap comes as a blessing in disguise to the victim who enjoys at the moment sanctifying grace. Suppose now his angel, knowing the waywardness of the man, could see for him in the future no better prospect of beatitude: would it not have been a false act of mercy to prevent the beneficial accident? The designs of an all-wise Providence, which the angels understand, become to us, on account of their being unknown, a meritorious test of faith. St. Ambrose was of the opinion, and confidently expressed it, that out of his very solicitude an angel may suspend his aid so that a stalwart soul will gain that much more merit by overcoming temptation without it.

But make no mistake! The eloquent eulogist of angels is not in the least recommending a spirit of indifference toward them. "We should pray to the angels sent to us as guardians," he recommends. "Often think of them," St. Bernard likewise admonishes, "and devoutly pray to them who guard and console you at every moment." We must rely on their available help. Only, the reliance is not to exclude our cooperation. People who relax every effort and expect their angels to drag them into heaven are not going to get there. As the administrators of God's providence in the world, the angels respect the freedom which God has imparted to the human will.

Whether your angel belongs to this or that choir of the heavenly court, so long as you have him, remains no concern of yours. It is purely an academic curiosity. The classic *De coelesti hierarchia* has decided arbitrarily that guardian angels are chosen never from the higher but always from the lower ranks; specifically, from one of the three lowest: if not indeed, as some adherents of the theory insist, from the very lowest. "Not so!" argues back Duns Scotus, seeing no reason why guardian angels should not be drawn indiscriminately from any of the nine choirs.

Such mystics as St. Gertrude, St. Matilda, St. Hildegarde, and such scholars as Durandus and Tauler, agree with Scotus. A seraph who attends the All-Holy, they all felt, would not be demeaning his dignity if along with that he took care of a human soul. Why could he not blend the double duty into a unified harmony as any other guardian angel does? Does not man have to combine his love of God with love of neighbor? Neither is a distraction from the other.

Of no matter what choir, our guardian angel is to us the closest angel of heaven. An intimacy with one so benign, so powerful, so faithful, if cultivated, would pay off handsomely. It would avert those unnecessary spells of loneliness that sadden life. We simply cannot feel alone when thinking of, talking to, confiding in a companion who is always there to listen, who really cares, who all year round has no desire to take a vacation from our presence.

Of what human associate may that be said?

XII

Apparitions Have Made History

A NGELS ARE NOT A SIDE ISSUE in any proper study of man. Their influence on history has been enormous. Think of the difference to the world if none of them had ever advised the patriarchs or prophets of old; if Gabriel had not appeared to Mary; if none of the heavenly host had aided the apostles to get their mission off to a prodigious start. Their interventions have changed the course of history.

Is there sufficient reason to believe they have lost their active interest in the world? That, once Biblical times had passed, they have never shown their presence?

To maintain that angels have stopped appearing to mankind since the apostle John had his visions of them on the island of Patmos is equivalent to calling a select company of saints from then to now so many irresponsible liars. Francis of Assisi, in seclusion on Mount Alverna, confided to Brother Leo that one morning there a seraph, having the posture of a crucified body, had flown to him: is it credible that this most unpretentious of men, bearing as his affidavit the marks of the Crucified Savior on his own body, should have been lying? The choice of taking his word against that of an insensitive denier of his claim ought not to cost the faithful, one would like to think, a moment's hesitation.

If a self-announced visionary has only too often turned out to be a fraud, or been proved a psychopath, what of it? Neither an imposter nor a delusionist, and surely not a prejudice, should discredit the genuine visionary. Every reputable case merits a distinct appraisal: this is what the Bollandists, those level-headed hagiographers, have accorded the known non-Biblical angelophanies from the second century on. They have studied them, one by one, sifting the evidence.

The comprehensive survey is to be found in their *Acta Sanctorum* under the date of September 29, formerly the feast of St. Michael exclusively (although its liturgy did pay honor to Michael's fellow angels as well). Why was the survey inserted here? Because there seemed to be no better place, since St. Michael's outnumber the apparitions of all the other angels together.

The story of Fatima, with its relevancy to the cruel times, affords a test. It embarrasses our sophisticates. But their discomfiture, however acute, does not invalidate the story. William Thomas Walsh did his authenticated version of it, to mention only one, from the four written but unpublished memoirs of Lucia after he had consulted her in her convent. He went to the source.

In all, the angel who appeared to the children of Fatima did so three times in 1916: to invite them to pray with him to the Blessed Trinity; to urge them to offer sacrifices for the repentance of sinners; to give them, from the ciborium he carried, Holy Communion. In his references to the Sacred Heart of Christ, the boyish-looking angel of great splendor always included the Immaculate Heart of Mary. His apparitions were but a prelude to hers, which were to follow on six well-spaced occasions the next year and which were to outshine his own radiance to the ecstatic delight of her three little confidants.

May Francisco, who did not hear but only saw, be properly called a confidant? Why not? He could hear, if not the glorious Lady with the rosary, at least Lucia replying to her: and from both Lucia and Jacinta he would then learn what she had said to them. So had it been with the earlier apparitions. The boy could only see the angel, and when the angel prayed aloud with the three of them, Francisco had to take his words from the lips of the girls, which by the grace of God he did with an effortless joy.

Need one believe in the apparitions of Fatima? That depends. If you are convinced of their authenticity, and that God has thus chosen to speak to the world through the Mother of his Divine Son, then the obligation is there to accept them. The revelations made to the children at Fatima, it is true, do not fall into a class with defined dogma. Private revelations never do. Their credibility relies on the evidence that supports them.

And that's the whole point here. The sanctions upon the message of Fatima, honestly examined, are of the strongest inducement to anyone not adverse to the supernatural. They have a cumulative force which, to an open mind, encourages assent. Aside from the prime consideration that the children under a constant harassment had no likely motive to stick to their story if it were false, there remains so much else to recommend it.

Our Lady of Peace, following the angel of peace, appeared just at that point of time when the atheist revolution was about to break and her directives were most urgently needed, as only too soon the collapse of the League of Nations would prove. Equally telling, her predictions came true: that Jacinta and Francisco would die early, but that Lucia would survive to be her witness on earth; that the First World War would shortly end, but that a worse would succeed it if people did not stop their grievous sinning; that, still again, if her request for prayer and penance went unheeded, whole nations would be enslaved by an encroaching Communism and the intelligentsia along with lesser minds would be taken in by its wiles.

Impressive as all that is, the evidence reaches its climax in the miracle of the sun. Promised to the children as their guarantee of sincerity to the world, it did indeed occur before an estimated seventy thousand witnesses on the very date and hour of day that Our Lady had said it would. Having awaited it in a drizzle of rain, astounded by it to a point of consternation, the crowd was treated to a secondary miracle for good measure: they found their drenched clothing suddenly dry. But let that pass. It was the way the sun had acted that counts.

"A spectacle unique, and incredible if you had not been a witness to it," is how the Freemason editor of *O Seculo* summed it up. Confronted by an obvious miracle, some of the more sophisticated reporters described it with an ingenuity that got around using the forbidden word a single time. Not a hostile journal in Portugal dared deny it. There had been too many witnesses: the crowd at the Cova, to be sure, and even isolated others miles away; this promptly demolishes the silly supposition of mass hypnosis.

What exactly had the crowd seen? What did the sun do? When of a sudden the rain stopped and the clouds parted, there it shone, brilliantly, yet without dazzling or hurting the eyes, and it held its usual place in the sky. A moment later, it was dancing crazily. Then it began to whirl, like a resplendent wheel going around at a dizzy pace and spreading the brighest rays of light over the sky in a variety of hues: green, red, orange, yellow, blue, violet, and the rest. The Cova, its trees, its rocks, the people present, all reflected as well as the clouds that rich succession of hues.

After a while, the furious spinning halted, only to resume within a brief interval, and to fling out again its gorgeous display of fireworks, if that is the word. Three times had the sun thus revolved and stopped. Then the fiery disc gave a violent shudder, and plunged angrily it seemed, zigzagging wildly, toward the crowd.

The crowd gasped, quaked with terror. Many fell to their knees to call out to God for mercy. All thought it was the end of the world. Those who had come to jeer did not jeer. And when to the crowd's great relief the sun recovered its normal position in the sky, none was in any mood to question the power of that invisible hand which had made good beyond the wildest expectation the promise given to the children.

The message of Fatima, besides its recommendation from such evidence, has something else going for it. It has, short of a *de fide* proclamation, the approval of the Church. The liturgy, taking Our Lady of Fatima seriously, has incorporated into its cycle of feasts one to the honor of her Immaculate Heart. More than that, on the first Saturday of every month, it ordinarily allows a Votive Mass under the same title. Still not satisfied, Pope Pius XII added yet another feast to Mary's honor: that of Mary, Queen of the World. Nor did he keep the reason to himself. "The time for doubting Fatima," he declared, "has passed. It is now time for action."

Action from him there certainly was. On July 7, 1952, he consecrated the Russian people, and all the world, to the Immaculate Heart of Mary. On November 12, 1954, he raised to the rank of a minor basilica the Church of Our Lady of the Rosary at Fatima, "where lie buried the bodies of Francisco and Jacinta Marto, *who were favored with a wonderful vision of the Mother of God.*" Previous to this, in 1951, he even closed the Holy Year in Fatima, not Rome, and on October 13 at that, the thirty-fourth anniversary of the miracle of the sun. Not there in person, the Holy Father had a special delegate at the shrine to represent him.

But he spoke for himself to the vast assemblage. Radioed from Rome into the amplifiers around the Cova da Iria, his voice had never sounded more vibrantly alive than when it emphasized to a hushed audience the importance of Our Lady's peace plan of prayer and penance, with her loving insistence on the daily rosary. It was a noteworthy ceremony throughout. The crowds, many of whom had walked long distances to the shrine, were such that only a percentage of them could jam into the spacious esplanade. Yet, to the credit of the amplifiers, those closed out were not shut off from the Pope's message.

"The most spectacular thing I've ever seen," said Andrew Gold of the scene. "If we made it in Hollywood, nobody would believe it." But the cameraman for Warner Brothers, interested in what the eye could see, did not see to the heart of the matter. Frank Conniff did. "If the roots of faith strike so deep," he concluded his dispatch to the American Newspaper Syndicate, "there is no reason to believe that they do not still endure in countries under Communist domination. . . . When we tote up the assets of the free world, this persevering faith in Christlike values cherished by millions of ordinary Europeans may be more important to our side than the weight of their military power."

On another of these solemn occasions at the shrine, May 13, 1956, another legate represented Pope Pius: the man who would very soon himself occupy the Chair of Peter. And on that occasion, having first described the miracle of the sun, what did Cardinal Roncalli have further to say to the packed crowds at the Cova? He said that our dying Savior, having committed us to the custody of his mother, seemingly wanted her to show us her solicitude "even corporally, now here, now there, in womanly form. Thus can her apparitions be explained in the history of the Church."

Pope John XXIII, a devotee who, according to his *Journal of a Soul,* prayed all fifteen decades of the rosary every day of his later life, surprised only those who did not really know him when he called Fatima "the center of Christian hopes." His successor would seem to share the conviction. At the recent Council he consecrated the world anew to the Immaculate Heart of Mary, and immediately stated his intention of sending to Mary's shrine in Fatima as a token of his personal esteem the Golden Rose.

It is there now. It bears its own explanation why. Its inscription, translated into English, would read: "Pope Paul VI, imploring the protection of the Mother of God upon the whole Church, dedicates this Golden Rose to the Sanctuary of Fatima, May 13, 1965."

Pope Paul himself later went to Fatima on "a pilgrimage of prayer and penance" and "in the interest of peace," he said, to officiate at the Golden Jubilee, May 13, 1967. He offered an outdoor Mass, preached the homily, led the Prayer of the Faithful in a series of multilingual petitions that tranquillity might come at last to our strife-weary generation. He posed alongside Lucia, the happiest of nuns, to face the million in attendance and other untold millions of television witnesses. The Holy Father, in his every move, was publicizing to the world his unshaken belief in Fatima. He was but showing himself a devout client of Mary, who would work for peace her way.

As for the angel of peace who had predisposed the three young shepherds in the summer of 1916 for the later apparitions of Mary, he had a luminous beauty, the appearance of a youth in his mid-teens, and a manner that enthralled. His radiance looked, to Lucia, who dictated her impression to William Thomas Walsh in her own language, "more brilliant than a crystal penetrated by the rays of the sun."

"The words of the angel," Lucia has written, "were like a light which made us understand who and what God really is; how he loves us and wishes to be loved. The value of sacrifice was for the first time clear. Suddenly we knew its appeal to God and its power to convert sinners. From that moment we began offering to him all that mortified us, all that was difficult or unpleasant, except then we did not seek extra sacrifices and penances as we later learned to do."

Who was this gorgeous angel of heaven? He may have been, and is generally considered to be, St. Michael. He announced himself as the angel of peace, which happens to be his title in one of the hymns proper to his feast. This indomitable foe of evil, which underlies all turmoil, is hailed in the chant as the restorer and champion of peace.

Of the more famous angelophanies known to history outside the Bible, St. Michael figures in almost all. He has to his memory some noteworthy shrines around the world, architectural wonders, which mark the site of his apparitions. Among these, the Michaelion at Sosthenion, about fifty miles south of Constantinople, now Istanbul, must surely be counted. The Emperor Constantine the Great, credited with having seen the archangel, had the church erected to him in an act of gratitude. So the fifth-century historian Sozomen would have us believe. Attracting pilgrimages from far and wide, the Michaelion soon became a refuge of the sick: and history must admit, however it may explain, that through the centuries many of the medically incurable have returned from the shrine cured.

We needn't wonder that an angel appeared to Constantine. He had seen another vision, an insignia and message aglow in the sky, which has behind it a mass of evidence not to be explained away. Philostorgius, Nicephorus, Gelasius, Zonaras, the Emperor Leo, Brentius, Rivetus, Nazarius, Lactantius, Rufinus, and the Christian author Socrates, have all dealt with the event. Eusebius of Caesarea, a confidant of Constantine, has even elaborated upon it. Pagans vied with Christians to testify to its reality.

With an entire army of witnesses, and dozens of reporters, it could be expected that a diversity of detail would get into the reports. As for that, Constantine, for whom the miracle was chiefly intended, may have been given more to see than his soldiers.

He may have seen shining to him from the heavens, as the Emperor Leo insists, not only a cross but the monogram ☧ [1] and beneath them, spelled out in letters no less brilliant, the inscription: *In this sign conquer.*

Aptly does Cardinal Newman observe, "If in matter of fact our Lord was then really addressing Constantine, it seems trifling to make a grave point that he did so in this way, and not in that."

Those who reject supernatural intervention in human affairs will, of course, tolerate no evidence in its favor. They presume that miracles do not occur. But they only assert the impossibility; they do not prove it. They cannot prove it. Since the archangel Michael has never appeared to them, nor the sky shown them a flaming cross with a message, who are they to say that nothing of the kind could have happened to the Emperor Constantine? In his book devoted to the theme, Newman concludes that "Christian miracles are attested by evidence even stronger than can be produced for any of those historical facts which we firmly believe." Somerset Maugham, though an agnostic, would agree. In *A Writer's Notebook* he says, "The miracles of Catholicism are as well authenticated as those of the New Testament."

---

[1] First two letters of the name *Christ* in Greek, which, after his great victory, Constantine ordered to be placed on the labarum.

As Dr. Alexis Carrel found out, however, evidence is only wasted on the prejudiced who repudiate it. His fellow scientists expelled him from their select family at Lyons for no other reason than that he sent to Lourdes, having exhausted the resources of medicine, a naturally incurable patient who came back cured. This victim of so intolerant a decision, who went on to distinguish himself at the Rockefeller Foundation and to win the Nobel prize, could not understand the inconsistency of his bigoted colleagues who boasted of their open-mindedness. It is not easy to understand. But we may as well get used to it; we live in a climate that fosters a denial of the miraculous, an age that has given the denial the status of a dogma.

Nonetheless, the mind has the right and uses its right to question the negation. Who should know better than St. Joan of Arc, whose trial has established her sincerity and sanity, whether or not she had apparitions of St. Michael? How would a skeptic disprove them? Do not the historic exploits that followed the angel's instructions favor a supernatural aid of the kind? How else would a simple country girl, still in her teens, have achieved national feats of valor and a military leadership unmatched in history? Do not her sensational predictions, which came true, verify her heavenly promptings? How are we to explain her identifying without hesitation the Dauphin Charles, whom she had never seen, when he was purposely disguised as just another of the many courtiers at court? Is hers, or that of her disclaimers, the saner explanation of the warrior-maid from Domremy?

Her heinously unjust trial proved the guilt of only her judges. She made them look bad. Having nothing to hide, nothing to tell but the truth, she gave them replies that stung their arrogance. How did she who was never in heaven know her voices were those of St. Michael, St. Catherine, St. Margaret? The voices told her so. Whose did she hear first? St. Michael's. Did she see him, too? Yes, and many other angels of heaven who accompanied him. "I saw them with my bodily eyes as well as I see you, and when they left me I wept."

She had wanted them to take her with them. They were a flock of angels of such beauty, and Michael by the way he spoke had been such a comfort, and by contrast our coarse world so misunderstood her, that she would not have been human not to weep when the vision faded from her. She saw the archangel repeatedly. However, in her curt replies to a biased court, St. Joan did not particularize her description of his glowing presence. She wouldn't afford her pompous bullies the satisfaction.

The influence of her apparitions on history, who can measure? Certainly the most important of her voices was the angel's. Without his guidance of

Joan, the future of Europe could not have been the same.

Nor, without its Constantine the Great, would the Roman Empire have turned out to be what it became. Would the emperor have had the strength to form his sprawling provinces into a united Christendom without the encouragement of his visions? How much did his angelic apparition mean to him? The magnificent Michaelion which he built in commemoration, I should think, holds the answer.

As for the angel who introduced Our Lady of Fatima to her visionaries, and who may have been Michael, he only opened the story Our Lady has yet to complete. Future historians may have cause to ascribe the unnecessary turmoil of the times to the neglect of this message.

XIII

Their Shrines Befit the Angels

S T. MICHAEL now and again appears, not as at Fatima, but as a warrior clad in armor, resolute in his young and vigorous maturity. Gregory the Great saw him thus, sheathing his sword. Tradition thinks of him so. Art so portrays him.

Indeed, a lofty statue of him as a warrior looks out on the Atlantic from atop the pinnacle of the abbey church built to his name on his own Mont-Saint-Michel. The statue is of a superb workmanship. A bronze figure lifting high its gleaming sword, spreading upward its great wings, trampling under an iron shoe the writhing and ugly form of Satan, it rises some 498 feet into the sky. It deserves a more exclusive attention than it is likely ever to obtain because of a magnificent disadvantage. It stands there, despite its eminence, a mere detail topping a massive harmony of stone that has repelled storms of oceanic violence, to remain after centuries of such endurance a supreme envy of architecture.

The present structure, with its mighty sweep of walls, buttresses and flanks in a graceful ascent to the most graceful of spires, needed five centuries from 1023 to reach completion. What a monument to Norman genius! Nowhere else can there be found a combination of Gothic and Romanesque done in unerring style to such a delicacy of finish. And the achievement, to add to its enormity, entailed the necessity of hauling all those innumerable blocks of heavy granite from the mainland to the sea, then piling them on barges to be floated to the isle, and once there hoisting them by hand to their lofty place in the rising edifice.

The construction no less than thirteen times encountered a disheartening setback. Or was it really ever disheartening? The damage the thirteen outbreaks of fire caused the unfinished workmanship only stirred in the Normans a determination to repair the loss on a grander scale. And they always did. Their devotedness to St. Michael, in whose honor they wrought to completion their answer to his request, has to be considered a marvel of no mean quality itself.

The archangel had asked for a shrine. He got an architectural chef-d'oeuvre. The event that inspired the colossal masterpiece dates back, three centuries before its foundations were laid into that solid cone of rock standing out of the sea, to the year 708. The archangel appeared in a vision to Bishop Aubert of Avranches, now a canonized saint, to state his request. He even picked the site.

And from then on the islet began gradually to be called Mont-Saint-Michel. Its first modest shrine amounted to no more than a whisper compared to the strong aspiration of faith which the present wonder of soaring stones and spire raises to the heavens. Yet, already in the lesser effort, the people were showing a willingness to meet the angelic challenge to their devotion as best they could. To this day, at the base of the Mount, barely out of reach of the tides, stands St. Aubert's Chapel, not indeed the original one but its successor, which was built in the fifteenth century.

The Mount forms an isle off the coast of Normandy, which during the sea's lowest ebb becomes a peninsula. Yet even then, on account of the drifted sand, its only practical approach remains the mile-long causeway from the mainland. Normally, the circumference of its strand reaches around the isle to a proximate length of twelve miles. But about the time of the vernal equinox, the tides, the strongest known to Europe, rush in upon the shore in their high turbulence to lash at the lower buildings on the Mount and to render impassable the causeway itself.

Notwithstanding the difficult approach, the crowds who used to sail in at high tide now come in by the causeway, often a congested bottleneck of traffic to and from. Still, they come. The Mount averages 500,000 tourists a year. Nor does the footing become easier, once the islet has been reached. Here the arrivals must climb the narrow, winding, cobblestoned *Grande Rue,* not infrequently having to push through a mass of faster-moving pedestrians on their return down. This street, having admitted only pedestrians, leads to yet another difficult stage in the ascent: to a spiral outside stairway that goes steeply round the ramparts to the abbey and its entrance at last. It is a tiring experience. But the rewards amply repay the effort. Where is there an alternative attraction quite like St. Michael's lofty citadel in the sea?

The crowds were exceptionally large in the summer of 1966. That was because the thousandth anniversary of the abbey was then going on. To commemorate the arrival of Benedictine monks from Monte Casino at Mont-Saint-Michel all that time ago, the French government had marked off a period of thirteen months for national observance, from early September of 1965 to mid-October the following year. More than that, the authorities in Paris invited back to the long-vacated abbey a Benedictine community to reside there during the jubilee and, of course, conduct the liturgical ceremonies.

The festivities, in accord with the times, started with an ecumenical conference at the Mount. The discussions featured, as an incentive to unity, the theme of "Angels in the Judeo-Christian Tradition." St. Michael, to be sure, dominated attention. And his September feast that year, 1965, as again the next, was the occasion of the most elaborate of ceremonies at his appreciative abbey. But don't think for a moment that the other angels were slighted; they were not! St. Raphael, certainly, on his feast a month later, was honored with a Mass that, if not more solemn, obtained a greater publicity than St. Michael's: it was telecast from the Mount to all Europe this side of the Iron Curtain.

Mont-Saint-Michel must not be thought, from its tendency to monopolize attention, to be the only impressive summit dedicated to the prince of angels. Mountain climbers almost anywhere in Germany are likely to come across a chapel of St. Michael on some high ridge or other. In the ages of faith Europe was extremely fond of setting up his shrines where the land rose sharply to a superb eminence. Is it because the archangel himself has seemed to prefer the heights? His famous apparition to St. Laurence, a sixth-century bishop of Siponto, in a cave on Mount Gargano, which has a local feast to its memory on May 8, surely explains the imposing basilica now standing there in its pride of place. It is one of the artistic curiosities of southern Italy.

Its portals, brought from Constantinople, feature angelic representations from the Old and New Testaments: the angel saluting Mary, the angel counseling Joseph, the angel with Joshua, the angel carrying the prophet Habakkuk by the hair to Daniel, the angel staying the hand of Isaac, the angel wrestling with Jacob, the angel delivering Peter from jail, and the angels of Easter morning sitting by the empty tomb. The prince of angels has his portrayals, and prominent ones, inside the basilica. Pilgrims to the shrine always say they are going to St. Michael's Mountain.

The English have their St. Michael's Mount, too. It lies off the coast of Cornwall. Didn't John Milton refer to it in his threnody? But what most commentators fail to mention is that "the great Vision of the guarded Mount" alludes to the archangel's apparition there, which prompted the natives to confer upon the mountain its sacred name. The poet in fancy sees the angel still facing out to sea and implores him to look homeward, where his attentions are sorely needed.

While St. Michael has many additional memorials, such as the Castel Sant'Angelo near the Tiber and his scattered group of some fifteen shrines built in the old city of Constantinople, the other angels are not without theirs either. How many uncounted chapels, churches, cathedrals, how many public institutions of sundry kinds, are named after St. Gabriel? How many, again, have St. Raphael for their patron? And the Holy Angels without discrimination, without name — are they not everywhere represented? An oratory doesn't have to bear the title of Holy Angels to have its frescoed ceiling or walls, its stained-glass windows, alive with clusters of the heavenly beauties.

A preeminent shrine, Santa Casa di Loreto, the Holy House of Loreto, honors not only the Holy Family but also the holy angels. It has the best of reasons to honor them. They are said to have carried the revered little house, now enclosed in the larger ornate basilica, all the way from Nazareth. It had been the home of the Holy Family. And because it had, an inscription at the entrance to that outer basilica, if translated into English, would read: "Let those who are impure tremble to enter this sanctuary. The whole world has no place more sacred. This building is even holier than St. Peter's Basilica. . . . No place is more holy."

Another prominent inscription, to be found on the eastern façade, would in English read: "Here Mary most holy, Mother of God, was born; here she was saluted by the angel; here the Eternal Word of God was made flesh. Angels conveyed this house from Palestine."

For this service the angels are richly represented in the artistic work so evident in the Basilica of Loreto. Under construction for better than a century, having had designers of genius, and the best craftsmen available to execute the designs, the finished edifice with its broad dome completely encloses the Holy House. And its angels, frescoed to the dome, sculptured into watchful poses here and there in the larger building, may be said to keep watch over the smaller shrine in their midst.

Did the angels really deliver the Holy House to Loreto? It is a question which the enormity of the claim naturally invites. But the claim has its wealth of indirect evidence that amounts to a confirmation. First of all, from the time its transportation is reputed to have occurred, the Holy House has been missing from its old foundations in Nazareth. These remain there intact, to this day. They can be seen by any tourist to the Basilica of the Annunciation which enshrines them. And their measurements fit exactly the base of the Holy House of Loreto which has never rested on new foundations sunk into the earth, yet has enjoyed the firmest stability. Moreover, its interior walls, untouched in their original ruggedness, are of a stone and mortar not found in Italy but commonly found in Galilee.

The long succession of popes, from Julius II on, have in many a bull or brief identified in the most declarative of terms the Santa Casa di Loreto with the Holy House of Nazareth. They had no doubt of it. Three of them who had gone to the shrine ailing beyond any natural hope of recovery, left in good health; they were Pius II, Paul II, and Pius IX; their cures were admitted by competent medical authority to be miracles. In our own day, October of 1962, as may be recalled from his telecast close-up, Pope John XXIII knelt in the Holy House of Loreto to invoke heaven's aid upon the forthcoming Ecumenical Council. "On the vigil of the Second

Vatican Council the humble successor of Peter is here," he announced with an informal smile, and counted himself just another of the many faithful pilgrims who in the past four hundred and seventy-some years had preceded him to the shrine.

Pope John was alluding not only to his predecessors in office, but to the great saints as well who had for this shrine an insatiable attachment. If he singled out for special mention Charles Borromeo, and then Francis de Sales, it was because he considered them typical of the rest: Ignatius Loyola, for instance, and Alphonsus Liguori, and Francis Xavier, and such a multitude of devout women as to discourage any attempt to enumerate them. Anna Catherine Emmerich, the heroic stigmatist who could not travel, so much wanted to see the Holy House that she was granted by the grace of Providence a mystic vision of it. Had that holiest of homes arrived at Loreto before Francis of Assisi died in 1226 (it arrived late that same century), who can doubt that it would have known another devotee and one of its most frequent visitors?

None of the saints who ever spoke or wrote of it doubted that the angels had brought it from Nazareth. They didn't find the tradition hard to believe. They knew the ways of heaven. Since the house had stood in danger of raids which occurred in the area from time to time, why shouldn't the angels have seen to it that no pillagers would get their hands on this most venerable of homes?

It would be nothing more than what anyone familiar with the Bible might expect of the angels. If there is something extravagantly amusing to the imagination, that a flight of angels picked up a house from its foundations and whisked it off to a safer country, so again does it raise a smile to read of the prophet Habakkuk's being grabbed by the hair and delivered through the air to the lion's den. Angelic interventions are matter-of-fact occurrences in Old and New Testaments.

The Acts of the Apostles, dealing with the spread of the faith, might be called a monument built of words to the angels as much as to the missionaries whom they assisted. When the Ethiopian eunuch required someone to explain the Scriptures to him as he rode along reading, it wasn't long before Philip was in the carriage with him: an angel had arranged the meeting between the apostle and his immediate convert.[1] When the centurion Cornelius sent for Peter to baptize him, the first of the Gentiles to receive the sacrament, it was an angel who had planned the whole affair.[2] Thus the story goes, one angel appearing here, another there, to meet the needs of the moment.

A readiness to do God's bidding has earned for the angels their very name. They carry messages to

---

[1] See Acts 8:26ff.   [2] See *ibid*. 10:22ff.

earth with an unerring fidelity to the divine will: and when on their errands they adopt a human body they show it off to best advantage. Not a known visionary who has tried to describe an angel clothed in human splendor but admits the inadequacy of words to do such beauty justice. The angels deserve the shrines and monuments which their apparitions have won for them from a grateful humanity.

There stands in a public square of Barcelona a statue commemorating its guardian angel. St. Vincent Ferrer, approaching the city one day, had a vision of him, and later in church, in the pulpit, related to the assembly his experience. He said that he had just met an angel outside who was the most beautiful person in Barcelona and who introduced himself as its special guardian. The announcement started a sensation that spread like a raging fire through the city. It brought prompt action, and as soon as the sculptor could put his finishing touches to it, the citizens had their requested angel standing out in the open on permanent display.

Art, whether it builds shrines or molds statues or paints pictures or writes songs in their honor, is only expressing a gratitude which humanity owes the angels. It is simply repaying them for favors received. But it can never return a full payment. The angels have done us too many favors for art to manage that.

XIV

Art Advertises the Angel

IF TO THE POET FROST butterflies "are flowers that fly and all but sing," angels are, to every branch of art, great human birds that do both.

The poet blurts out a seeming inaccuracy only to take a shortcut to the truth. When these bright insects on the wing really do look like flowers flying about like birds and as if at any moment they too might break out singing, one cannot do quicker justice to the honest observation than by just such a play to the imagination, which doesn't have to stop to explain because it isn't necessary. It is not a question of sacrificing the strict definition to a metaphor, but of gaining a better understanding, a quick insight.

In much the same way, and for the same purpose, does art behave toward the angel. It takes metaphorical liberties in order to do him justice. It shapes him to human form, not because the angel is not good enough as he is, but because we cannot otherwise understand him. To be told that an unseen spirit of higher intelligence than ours is still a person like us, though accepted on faith, does not impress. We do not actually feel the kinship until art pictures the lofty spirit to us as a recognizable cousin. That it adds wings to his back and may even put a song on his lips, is done only to ensure at the same time his ethereality and his membership with the heavenly choirs.

Art by its every gesture aids, rather than embarrasses, angelology.

The embarrassments come, when they do, by sheer accident. Yet come only too frequently they do. Who hasn't in church seen statues of grinning cherubs that belie to the extreme the great angelic beauty they are supposed to represent? They are nothing less than a hideous mistake. But that rather means they hadn't been so intended; they simply did not turn out according to design; unless by an outside chance their molders or cutters were adept infidels with a sardonic sense of humor. In which case, the malicious result could still not invalidate the ideal it mocks. Nor does any unintentional injustice to it diminish its proven worth. Art has done nobly well by the angels.

And angels owe their popularity to art. Once Holy Scripture had brought them to the world's attention, and theology explained them, it was art that kept reminders of them before the public eye. Just reminders to the eye? It sings of them, too. It even lets them do the singing. How many celebrated composers have set to music Gabriel's sublime announcement to Mary? How many oratorios have accorded their angels the honor of important solos? *The Dream of Gerontius,* for one, does more. Its alternate chant between this voice and that yields now and again to a torrential onrush of sound as there comes crowding into the ear, out of heaven, the multitudinous harmony of the angelic choirs.

Art, humanizing its angels, often has them singing. Why shouldn't it have? Their business in heaven is to praise God. And for another good reason art gives to its angels, along with fine singing voices, a never-aging youth. You never see one of them showing up in art, or the Bible, as a bearded old gentleman in need of a cane. Such enfeeblement would outrage his spiritual agility, which calls for a quick mobility of form and a strong pair of wings rather than a staff. Any symbol, to be worth its choice, must in some appreciable way suit whatever reality it represents.

Thus, understandably, did the nineteenth-century artist who would stress angelic beauty over angelic power feminize his angels. He preferred to work from models who would make fit candidates in a beauty contest. Something there was about the Victorian climate that favored this shift of fashion. Nor has the trend come to an end in commercial art. Statuaries turn out such angels by the carload. Stationery stores sell them, depicted on Christmas or Easter cards, by the boxes.

Very many still want their angels of a kind that Charles Dickens once recommended. Himself all

for it, he was inclined to believe that God was, too.
"The younger lady," he writes of Rose Maylie in
Oliver Twist, "was in the lovely bloom and spring-
time of womanhood; at that stage when, if ever
angels be for God's purposes enthroned in mortal
forms, they may be, without impiety, supposed to
abide in such as hers."

What the feminine angel of today, slender of
form, does retain from the past is the old dignified
decency of attire. This is as it should be. Bold
styling, designed to exercise an appeal extraneous
to the angelic nature, would only offend it. There
are limits beyond which no wise artist goes. The
genuine craftsman, with his instinct for good taste,
practices restraint.

That nineteenth-century art swung away from the
virile type of angel, and that really some of the
earlier masters had made the break when they created the child-angel with the miniature wings, are
both of them innovations of debatable merit. C. S.
Lewis, while conceding some merit to "the chubby
infantile nudes of Raphael," dismisses the effemin-
ate Victorian angel as totally insipid. He longs for
a return to Fra Angelico's fine, strong creations,
who "carry in their face and gesture the peace and
authority of heaven." He rates Dante's characterizations of angels, however, better still — the best in
art. They have a majesty, a sublime awfulness which

those of the Bible, Lewis believes, invariably show.
He has a point.

But the point admits of exceptions which Lewis
seems to have missed. The first of the Christmas
angels in the sky, brightening it to an unexpected
glory, had indeed so frightened the shepherds that
they had to be told not to fear. Nine months earlier,
the mother-to-be had herself to be told, by the angel
of the Annunciation, not to fear. Daniel, like the
guards at the tomb, fainted at the mere sight of an
angel. Shock, there is no disputing it, is none too
strong a word to use of the normal reaction to
angelic visions within the extensive confines of
Scripture.

But not every Biblical angel inspires the terror
of awe. Raphael did not. The angel who freed
Peter from prison went unrecognized as one until
they parted. It is a false premise to assume that
the angel of art ought always to inspire awe because
the angel of Scripture always does.

The angel of Scripture does not. It depends on
the circumstances whether or not he awes: what the
reaction to him is to be. If the purpose of his visitation is to show off an angel's companionability, then
as a companion does he appear. If it is to announce
some formidable decree out of eternity, then as an
august messenger of the Lord he comes. Every angelic appearance is but an accommodation on the

part of the spirit to a human emergency: and the emergency alone dictates the particulars.

The angel whose brilliance hurt the eyes of St. Frances of Rome, so that she had to avert her glance, looked to be no older than her eight-year-old son, whom she had recently lost to death. The angel had come to assure her that the two of them were now associates in heaven. And with what consummate propriety did he not adapt his appearance to the circumstances! He could not have made the mother better realize his intimacy with her boy than by assuming a like age. He could not have better conveyed to the mother the glorification which her little son shared with him than by emitting a radiance so bright that it dazzled while it enthralled.

Sacred art has sufficient precedent for adopting innovations and subjecting them to its purposes. It certainly has the perfect sanction for making children of its angels when angels themselves have thus appeared. In the *Sistine Madonna,* as a kind of afterthought, the painter has worked in at the bottom of his picture two infantine cherubs, giving them faces of a mischievous but subservient charm. These youngsters look knowing, precociously amused. No one has to tell them which Infant in the picture rates supreme. Their inclusion needs no apology. It has enhanced a masterpiece.

Christmas may be said to have brought to art the baby-sized cherub. While the angels who sang to the shepherds remain in every form of art adults, those who cluster about the crib are often depicted scarcely old enough to be out of one themselves. Knowing who lies there, and that human infancy now exceeds their own dignity, they have come to pay their respects as fitting young helpmates of their God. It is a neat conception; and let who would, scoff, if this relieves him; but let him not think for a moment that he owns a monopoly on artistic standards.

Another favorite theme of art, which attracts flocks of these infant cherubs, is the Assumption. The reason is clear: the artist would thereby indicate their subserviency to Mary who, for all the eminence of angelic dignity, transcends it. And men of faith like Titian, Murillo, Poussin, when they reduced their angels to such miniature escorts of her majestic flight heavenward, were simply acknowledging the superangelic grandeur of her person. The heavenly youngsters in some portrayals fairly swarm about their captive Queen as they go rejoicing with her into the skies.

As creatures of sense, who have understanding, too, we best respond to an idea that takes help from a sensory presentation. One glimpse at a sunset, a single sparkle of the eye from the right face, a simple strain of music, will any of them contribute more to an appreciation of beauty than the strictest treatise from an unimaginative philosopher. So with art: it materializes the angel in order to bring out to us the abstract truths about him.

It gives him a human body to remind us of our likeness to him. It makes a child of him to bring out his innocence, or his agelessness, or his subserviency to the Madonna and her Child. It makes a musician of him, showing him with an instrument, to suggest his constant state of jubilee. It might even, to emphasize his superintelligence, reduce him to a youthful head with wings. Whatever art does to pictorialize the angel is done to convey some truth about him. What it does to him is done for him.

Art has been good to the angel. The publicity he receives from it, which costs heaven not a cent, has familiarized his name on earth. Every picture of him, every statue, every description, every hymn or song, whatever its artistic merit, does him honor. All are so many acts of faith in him, memorials to his reality.

XV

Angels of Art

O N EARTH the question leads only to disagreement. But it would be interesting to know from heaven, where harmony prevails, what angels of art the blessed there consider the best. Would they be Dante's? Fra Angelico's? Handel's? Michelangelo's? Or, if none of these, then exactly whose?

Or doesn't heaven care?

It surely cares that the arts have promoted faith in its angels, especially now that many are denying the angels' existence. But do the blessed in heaven go beyond that? Have they in mind a particular poet, painter, sculptor, composer, for having done the best angels in all art? On which artist from what art, if it came to that, would heaven confer the prize?

We cannot know.

And it does not matter. The fine arts, including wood carving as a form of sculpture, have vied with one another to their common benefit in a time-honored representation of angels: and that is what matters. Whether individual taste prefers the visual to the auditory, whether a connoisseur would sooner look upon Gerard David's earthward flight of angels

than to hear from Mozart how their *Gloria* sounded
to the shepherds on Christmas night is of no account.

What counts is, we have both the music and the
painting to enjoy.

The arts, interacting one upon the other, have
for that reason turned out better angels. And the
artist, far from resenting the rivalry, welcomes it.
"Giotto's all the rage today," acknowledges Dante
with a rhythm to match his enthusiasm. Indeed, in
the same *Cantica,* he pauses at a terrace on Mount
Purgatory to admire a work of art exquisitely cut
into the marble cliff. Was the poet imagining, or
only remembering what some fellow artist had done,
for he lived among great sculptors as well as great
painters?

> That angel, bearer of the great decree
> Which brought the long-desired peace on
>   earth,
> Reopening Heaven, closed by ancient ban,
> Was carved before us there in very truth,
> And shone in such a gentle attitude
> It seemed he scarce could be a silent image.
> One could have sworn that he was saying
>   *Ave!*

The Annunciation, as a favorite subject of religious art, enjoys a parity with Christmas and the
Assumption. In music, with the many *Ave Marias*

from gifted composers, it may even come first. It
at any rate accounts for the Angelus bell which at
its purest makes a daily melody of its own, authen-
tically sweet, amid the confusion of a discordant
world. Poets, listening, have quite a number of
them caught the message and gone away restless
until they could put it to verse.

> Ave Maria! blessed be the hour!
>   The time, the clime, the spot! where I so oft
> Have felt that moment in its fullest power
>   Sink o'er the earth so beautiful and soft,
> While swung the deep bell in the distant tower,
>   Or the faint dying day hymn stole aloft,
> And not a breath crept through the rosy air,
>   And yet the forest leaves seemed stirred
>   with prayer.

There is nothing here, in the reaction of Byron
to the Angelus and the evening hymn of the monks,
to surprise. It certainly did not surprise Pope John
that the Angelus theme created such an emotional
stir on earth, in or out of art. He was only dis-
appointed that the familiar appeal of the Angelus
no longer sounds from many a now silent belfry
in crowded cities which need it most. After all, the
angel's announcement to Mary "begins Christian
history . . . and deserves to be honored by bells
throughout the world three times a day." So wrote
Pope John XXIII.

Long before bells were doing it honor, shortly after the year 100, an unknown hand had frescoed to a wall of the Roman Catacomb of St. Priscilla the Angel's Errand to the Virgin Mary. Another mural of the Annunciation adorned the Catacomb of Sts. Peter and Marcellinus. In both pictures Gabriel has human form, without the wings.

Not until the fourth century, when the Emperor Constantine began erecting shrines, did the angels of Christian art take on wings. Thus, in the British Museum, one may see a bas-relief of St. Michael from the fourth century: the figure, neatly carved of ivory, has an exquisite pair of wings. And on the triumphal arch of St. Mary Major's in Rome the angel Gabriel has been painted in flight, soaring on the swiftest of wings toward Mary who, amid a cluster of attendant angels, is seated. The picture, dating from the fifth century, adds to the evidence that the angel of the Annunciation was a prime favorite of early Christian art.

Nor has he worn out his welcome. "The angel and the girl are met," begins a recent poem of unaffected simplicity, devoid of ornament, reverent in tone. The poem has, in the judgment of Horace Gregory, "an air of eternal freshness, an early-Christian touch and truthfulness that Giotto's frescos have." And since the author's better work all shows the same purity of execution, the critic thinks that

Edwin Muir may yet prove to be the most enduring of contemporary poets.

When a poet has some quality about his verse that reminds his reviewer of Giotto, he rates high. The father of Italian painting, and a worthy sculptor besides, has not lost his prestige since Dante's day. As recently as December of 1966 the Italian government issued a postal stamp showing his multicolored *Madonna Enthroned among the Angels*. The artist has indeed so many angels to his credit in striking frescos, at Assisi, at Padua, at Florence, and elsewhere, that nothing short of a book could describe them all. It is at Padua, in the Franciscan Chapel, that his *Annunciation* is to be found. There, on those privileged walls, Giotto painted a full series of scenes from the life of Jesus and Mary. Naturally, to have done that with any degree of fidelity to truth meant the inclusion of angels proper to the scenes.

Ruskin in a letter to Stacy Marks notes of Giotto and Fra Angelico, that to posterity they "left eternal monuments of the divinely blazoned heraldry of Heaven." It is true, of both. Their work still appeals. But of the two, Fra Angelico has produced the more authentic angel. His type of angel, while human in form, and beautiful, and strong, and clad in some material that might have been woven of the dawn, breathes of a spirituality that excludes the least hint of sex, although the features are of an utmost delicacy. His Gabriel, having just stepped into the presence of the Virgin Mary, is shown in an attitude of approach, with wings poised upright, hands folded crosswise upon the breast, the fully enrobed figure bent reverently forward to suggest an incipient bow. It reveals a poise, above the human, of deferential eagerness. The angel, human only in form, complements a masterpiece.

This particular *Annunciation* hangs in the Prado Museum at Madrid. But Fra Angelico did another as good for the baptistery of a Cortona church. His workshop with his aid turned out a *Nativity,* the pride of the Metropolitan Museum of Art, which shows the first-arrived angels already alighted on the stable roof and another angel flying toward the stable, suggesting that others are on the way. Fra Angelico, unaided, did a *Resurrection,* now in London, which displays the risen Christ in a thicket of singing angels. He did an *Assumption,* no less replete with jubilant angels, which Mrs. John Gardner of Boston used to have in her residence; it is presumably still in the public rooms there. The Angelico angels have really circulated. Of his three pictures of the *Coronation of the Virgin,* which called for angels and got them in profusion, one is on display at the Louvre, another at St. Mark's Museum in Florence, the third in the Uffizi Gallery. The famous *Two Angels Kneeling on Clouds* belongs to Turin. And the Vatican, to bring to an abrupt end the interminable list, has in its keeping the much coveted *Madonna and Angels.*

The gifted Dominican, who never took up his brush to begin a day's work without first a prayer, did not find his lofty commitment an undue strain. He moved about in a heavenly atmosphere, his natural climate, and painted his angels with assiduous ease. They took form on his canvas as convincingly as on Dante's page because he lived on intimate terms with them. The ability to turn out his abundant masterpieces, all on religious subjects and of a quality unmatched in art, demanded more than genius. It had to be genius transfused with sanctity. When Giovanni da Fiesole joined the Dominicans, they gave him the most appropriate of names. Posterity would seem to think so. It knows him by no other.

But Fra Angelico, preeminent for the religious fervor of his paintings, was just one of many who chose only religious themes. It was then quite the common practice. The more representative artists of the day considered it a profanation of their talent to use it on the secular. The result shows an angelic dominance, after Christ and his mother, in that outstanding period of art.

Neither Michelangelo nor Leonardo da Vinci a century after Fra Angelico, it is true, hesitated to select for their adept treatment the profane subject. Yet, aside from the *Mona Lisa,* what specimens of their nonreligious may compare with their religious art? Michelangelo, as much the greatest sculptor of that day as the other was its greatest painter, has nothing whatever of his profane pieces to equal the incomparable *Moses,* the flawless *Pietà,* or his enormous fresco on the ceiling of the Sistine Chapel.

The great sculptor turned painter for no other reason than to fresco that ceiling. He did his complicated theme with an astonishing unity of design. But having practically finished his huge picture of Creation, the Fall, the Expectation of the Messiah, he still had a final challenge to meet. Because of the contour of the dome, little triangular spaces had had to be left unpainted: what should an artist do with them? What in fact did Michelangelo do with them? He painted in angels, with the prophets, and had them all pointing one direction — to the coming Redeemer. It was a happy expedient. Far from being mere fillers, they tightened the unity.

More than twenty years after he had finished the fresco, he was called on to paint the front wall of the same chapel. On it he did his *Last Judgment,* portraying within the multitudinous scene a group of angels carrying the symbols of the Passion. Come to think of it, wasn't it a sculptured *Kneeling Angel* which he did for the shrine of St. Dominic at Bologna that started him on his way to fame? He was only seventeen at the time. But the figure has a look of such pensive calm that one wonders how it could have been wrought in stone at all.

As an architect, Michelangelo in his eighties did his last great work. It was a prodigious undertaking. He converted a portion of the Roman baths of Diocletian into the Church of St. Mary of the Angels. He had once said of Fra Angelico: "The monk must have seen Our Lady to portray her so." Now had come his opportunity to honor her on a grand scale worthy of his genius. The old man made the most of it. A look inside the finished structure would find quick evidence that the church had a name that fits. Their Queen and the Angels, in a wealth of designs, abound.

Does anybody today speak of Buonarroti? Isn't he to everybody simply Michelangelo? One could wish that the hewer of his gigantic *Moses* had carved from another block of stone a statue of his namesake, the prince of angels. None could have executed it with a stronger finesse than the many-sided genius who even ornamented his personal copy of the *Divine Comedy* with marginal drawings of its angels. Would that so precious a copy had not been lost!

Just as Michelangelo's first considerable piece of work was a sculptured angel, so the painting that first drew attention to Leonardo was that of an angel he had done when still a youth at the Academy of Florence. His instructor, Andrea di Verrocchio, was himself doing the *Baptism of Christ* and allowed the pupil to try his hand on a contributory incidental. The incidental proved to be a standout. It paled to mediocrity the rest of the picture. It was one of the two boyish-looking angels in the design, the golden-haired one kneeling on the riverbank and holding our Lord's garments.

The oval face made more beautiful by that glow of golden hair, the interplay of light and shadow in the blue tints of the robe that enfolds the shapeliest of forms, brought the first taste of fame to the greatest painter of his generation. "This ravishing countenance," says Louis Gillet of the angel's face, "shines with a divine life." In this exquisite angel, the art historian and painter Giorgio Vasari says, "Verrocchio recognized a master hand." His own could not match it. The pupil had outdone his teacher.

Of the two Da Vinci pictures known by the title of *Virgin of the Rocks,* and almost identical in design, the second rates superior. It owes that superiority to its angel. Leonardo had left Mother and Child, and the landscape with its rocks, unfinished for an apprentice to touch up, which he did creditably well. But the apprentice could not achieve the precise delicacy of that unearthly angel kneeling so apparently alive before the Divine Infant. He is entirely Leonardo's. No one else put brush to him. He is worth going to the National Gallery to see.

The less masterful *Virgin of the Rocks,* on ex-
hibit in the Louvre, is by no means unimportant.
Only Fra Angelico seems to have been capable of a
perfect angel every time he attempted one. But Da
Vinci at his best merits comparison. He certainly
has a miniature Annunciation at the Louvre, in which
Gabriel shows a reverence that glows.

Their angels contributed no little to the reputation of great artists. Among the painters — along
with Angelico and Da Vinci — Titian, Andrea del
Sarto, Jan Van Eyck, Dürer have all been acclaimed
for their treatment of the Annunciation. Dürer did
not stop there, but went on to complete a series of
episodes from the *Life of the Blessed Virgin* which
could not have fulfilled its purpose without its angels. To disassociate the Queen of Angels from the
angels would be an incredible inanity.

Of the Assumption, Titian has done two masterpieces. In the one, which hangs in the Venetian
church of Santa Maria Gloriosa, Mary stands parti-
ally enwrapped in a cloud and encircled by a wide
ring of cherubs. The artist keeps them at a suitable
distance so as not to hide from view their triumphant
Queen. His other picture, in the cathedral of
Verona, has fewer but more distinct cherubs. It is
plain on their chubby faces that they are the proudest and happiest of youngsters for having come by
such a Queen. They look at you as if to say, writes
James Russell Lowell, "Did you ever see a Madonna

like *that?* Did you ever behold one hundred and fifty pounds of womanhood mount heavenward before like a rocket?"

Murillo also has two of the Assumption to his name, which are usually referred to as his Immaculate Conception pieces. El Greco has one. But why enumerate them all? Rubens did his Assumption for the cathedral in Antwerp, and Corregio his for the cathedral of Parma. And Perugino's, while it never got into a cathedral, might well have. The subject of angels making off into the empyrean with their Queen has fascinated art: and the fascination started early.

In a church dating from the fourth century, at Malamocco, near Venice, the tourist will find a picture to charm. The unknown artist has managed to convey an impression of hasty movement as the fluffy cloud sails upward with Mary, and she with outstretched arms and upturned face looks as if she were already seeing into heaven, while around her flies along an escort of angels, all adult, with folded hands or in other attitudes of profound reverence. That face of the Virgin Mother holds a radiance not of this world.

Her motherhood has made Mary a favorite of art. It has won her, in a hundred representations, the honor of a welcoming committee, flights of rejoicing angels to accompany her heavenward. Art is fond of her because of whose mother she is.

The Christ of art can be expected to have around him crowds of ministering angels. Albrecht Altdorfer is not satisfied, in his *Nativity,* to have an angelic choir in the sky; he must bring into the stable three cherubs and have them kneel around the crib with Mary, while Joseph stands to the side and the shepherds tarry in the doorway. Etching the *Flight into Egypt,* Domenico Tiepolo has angels hovering over the Child, watching him every step of the way as the donkey plods on, led by Joseph. Jan Gossaert depicts the evangelist Luke kneeling on a prie-dieu, not praying, nor writing, but painting the Infant Christ clasped to his mother's heart, surrounded by cherubs, while a full-grown angel of the largest wings looks over the artist's shoulder and with a hand on his guides the brush. This ingenious picture within a picture, which is now in the Museum at Vienna, shows two of the air-borne cherubs holding a precious crown directly over the Madonna, whose whole attention is given to the Child.

In art, from birth to death, and after his death, Christ has had the attention of angels.

Of the Crucifixion, Giovanni B. Castiglione has done a sketch in oil which omits the usual group of mourners at the foot of the cross to substitute a cluster of angels, some of them mere cherubs, hovering about the dying Savior. The cherubs are plainly heartbroken. One with a flap of his small wings has turned from the piteous sight, a hand covering his eyes. Another, looking on, stifles a sob. A third is rubbing his tearful eyes while his little mouth has opened wide in a vigorous wail. Two of them are pressing their lips to a riveted foot. And so on.

El Greco, you may be sure, put no cherubs in his *Crucifixion.* They were not his style. His two angels there are gigantic beauties, poised beneath the arms of the cross, their wings aflutter and their hands reaching out to the Crucified. Jesus, looking down at his mother, has just spoken the words entrusting her to his disciple John, who with her looks up at him. But Magdalene looks at Salome, John's natural mother, who in her astonishment looks nowhere in particular. The angels hovering above this bit of human drama are not concerned with it, only with their business of comforting the dying Christ. They bring to the unification of this picture based upon a Biblical text a tremendous poignancy.[1]

Isn't that what most of our religious art has done: taken some scriptural text and given it a portrayal? Guido Reni painted the angel who has come to release Peter from prison and who is telling him to "wrap your mantle around you and follow me." John Singleton Copley painted the two angels of the Ascension, who are saying: "This Jesus, who was taken up from you into heaven, will come in the same way as you saw him go into heaven." Rembrandt painted

---

[1] See John 19:26-27.

the angel wrestling with Jacob. He also etched an *Agony in the Garden,* showing the angel caressing the stricken Savior. Fra Angelico began his *Christ in a Glory of Angels,* and Signorelli completed it. They were both taking Jesus at his word: "Truly, truly, I say to you, you will see heaven opened, and angels of God ascending and descending upon the Son of Man."[2]

What liberties the artist takes with a text are taken only to emphasize its truth according to his personal realization of it. If you should have a copy of *The Christmas Story,* edited by the Metropolitan Museum of Art, get your hands on it if you will, and turn to page 18. There, in an important detail from Gerard David's *Nativity,* you will see come alive in color the familiar text: "And suddenly there was with the angel a multitude of the heavenly host praising God."[3] No two beauties in that descending choir of angels are alike. Each one of them wears a distinctive garb, his own pair of wings, and what he does with his hands, whether he folds them the way he does, or whether he spreads them out in an expansive gesture of good will toward men, is a study of the most graceful variety in harmony. Art does not distort, but interprets.

---

[2] Acts 12:7-11; *ibid.* 1:10-11; Gen. 32:24; Luke 22:43; John 1:51.

[3] Luke 2:13.

Any artist would paint wings on St. Mark's "young man"[4] at the tomb lest people mistake him for a human being. Fra Angelico, in fact, did. "I do not think," Monsignor Knox remarks with a sly touch of mischief, "there can be any doubt of St. Mark's young man being an angel." St. Matthew distinctly calls him one.[5]

But more than that, the artist is fond of these angelic wings for their own sake. He doesn't require much of a pretext to try his hand at them. As avidly as Dante in his writings, the painter or sculptor loves to depict or carve them to a meticulous finish. They serve him doubly: they satisfy an aesthetic urge in his soul and identify beyond a doubt the angels of a hundred museums, a thousand great cathedrals or churches.

Truly, nowhere so well as in the great cathedral do the arts combine in a common cause to achieve their highest grandeur. It is the proper home, far more so than the museum, for art's finest collection of angels. They are present there, in paintings, in mosaics, in wood carvings, in stained glass; they have been shaped from stone to attitudes of adoration to grace the sanctuary; and the music of the place becomes itself the jubilee of angels, adopting their very words, when a full chorus of voices joins

---

[4] Mark 16:5.

[5] See Matt. 28:5.

the mighty organ to fill the vast edifice with the praises of God.

And the edifice itself? What is such architecture, built so magnificently around the Real Presence, but a permanent echo of the angelic choirs? It is a serenade in stone to the Almighty. "Frozen music," the poet Goethe calls it. And so it is: a cantata, a symphony that never stops its *Gloria in excelsis Deo.*

More about Angels in Art

THE MEDIEVAL CATHEDRAL would naturally attract anyone who is looking for superb sculpture, the purest of stained glass, and a worthy percentage of the world's best painting. But the search should not be so restricted. Many another church, shrine or basilica, contains its share of the sublime in art. Mont-Saint-Michel, though not a cathedral, need not fear comparison with Chartres.

The art that built such hallowed showplaces left in them no dearth of angels. They are integral, not just ornamental, to the designing. They crowd the murals of the apse, support the pedestals, shine in the windows, flaunt their bright wings high up in the corners of the nave, even get into the mosaics of the pavement. And they haunt the portals of the façade, perch upon the turrets, add their beauty to the cornices, trample the devil into a writhing gargoyle. The problem, should anyone be so minded, would be to keep an accurate count of them all.

Ruskin once stood gazing rapturously up into a frescoed dome. It took his breath away, for the colors had been so blended and sharply defined as to "look like a cloud-wrapped opening in the seventh heaven, crowded with a rushing sea of angels."

How on earth, by what trick of the brush, did that arrangement of color convey a sense of so much depth, such action, such a vast but uncramped multitude of swift-flying angels in a space no wider in diameter than apparently thirty feet? Their numbers bewildered the man.

His experience was nothing unusual. The Romanesque style featured paintings of depth, massive to the eye, rich in design. Even the later Gothic structure, with its slanted roof and less mural space, was not devoid of them. Dorothy Sayers found to her delight the double hammer-beam roof of old St. Wendreda's Church in Cambridgeshire "alive with angels' wings." There, "flinging back the light in a dusky shimmer of bright hair and gilded wings, soared the ranked angels, cherubim and seraphim, choir over choir."

Ruskin, notably so, has enriched our literature with appreciations of the medieval cathedral. Yet, admiring it, proclaiming it the ideal in architecture, he does not penetrate to the secret of its magnificence. In his glowing reports he suffers a restriction upon his judgment. And in nothing does he more clearly betray his weakness, while lauding the cathedral, than in his response to its angels.

That he lavishes his praise upon them, heaven knows. He welcomes their representations in the murals, the windows, the statues, the medallions, wherever he finds them. He feels piously at home with them. But their purpose in the sanctuary, where they abound, somehow escapes him. He cannot seem to bring himself to believe, while admitting the beauty of their reverence, that they are there to adore Jesus in the Blessed Sacrament.

Chesterton summed it up in a sentence, if not precisely in these words, in words to this effect: John Ruskin admired everything about the medieval cathedral except the altar, which was why the cathedral was built in the first place.

It was, indeed. It could not otherwise have attained its magnificent unity. Its workers of no matter what craft brought to bear upon their effort a common dedication that has no equal in history. The master minds who did the planning, so long as their designs were carried out, did not fret over the likelihood of remaining anonymous to the future. The artisan, doing his tracery up on a cornice, where it might go unnoticed by man, did not on that account grow careless. He and the architect, the stonecutter, the glazier, the whole assembly of workers were all building a home for Christ: and because they were determined to make it as worthy of his divinity as they could, into it must go the most beautiful angels the human hand could shape.

Poetry, whose business it is to find and acclaim beauty, bows in humble acknowledgment:

Wilder than all that a tongue can utter,
Wiser than all that is told in words,
The wings of stone of the soaring gutter
Fly out and follow the flight of birds;
The rush and rout of the angel wars
Stand out above the astonished street.

Chesterton, as there indicated, had just the exuberance to understand that fine excess which, having no more room for angels inside, carved them to the exterior walls of the cathedral. He marveled that the façade "is thronged with open mouths, angels praising God, or devils defying him."

Angels are impartial to the divisions of art. They look good on canvas, in fresco, in mosaic, in sculpture. In the sanctuary fresco of Westphalia's Marian basilica they do their adoring nobly. They show well in a mosaic of the Assumption over a side porch of the Florence cathedral. The way they fold their hands to pray in the largest icon on earth, which hangs in the abbey church of Montevergine, gives the picture an unusual finesse. The group of *Christ and His Angels,* sculptured to the façade of St. Mark's in Venice, fascinates heart and mind as well as eye.

The sculptured angel enjoyed its finest period after Gothic had come into vogue. Then, in fact, the sculptor did little work independently of the architect. He didn't particularly want to mold a St. Michael for an isolated pedestal in some public park:

the objective was to get it into a cathedral, or out in one of its portals, even on a spire. The sculptor, like every other collaborator at the time, submitted his talent to the dictates of the architecture. To step into a medieval cathedral is not to be surprised by its massive harmony. A view of the exterior has already disposed the mind to expect it. Not a piece of bas-relief, none of the statuary, misfits. Every angel in the building belongs. Every detail contributes to the general effect.

The Milan cathedral, a Gothic miracle in white marble, has a total of six thousand statues carved in relief or in the round. None of them looks out of place. A third of the number stand outside, but, like those within, belong where they are. How many of them are angels? No statistician to my knowledge has taken the count. But they are considerable. In what cathedral are they not?

Whose hand, the question is often heard at Chartres, could have wrought out of a crude mass of stone such a clean-cut flight of angels going heavenward with such an ecstatic Queen? Yet there they are, a unit of figures, right over the main altar. To glance about, from this centerpiece, is to feel oneself hemmed in by the sublime. Nothing mars the effect. The sculptor, for all his contributions to the general sublimity, only worked along with the other artists, and they with him, to accomplish a perfect model of symmetry.

The painter was not idle here. Only now, with a sparsity of mural space available to him, he burned his colors into the windows. What was it Longfellow said of just such windows? His words, from the fourth sonnet of his series "Divina Commedia," are too relevant not to quote:

> I lift mine eyes, and all the windows blaze
> With forms of saints and holy men who died,
> Here martyred and hereafter glorified;
> And the great Rose upon its leaves displays
> Christ's Triumph, and the angelic roundelays,
> With splendor upon splendor multiplied.

The windows at Chartres, a hundred and forty-three in number, remain the most exquisite display of stained glass in Europe, which is tantamount to saying the world. The oldest pictorial window to survive the ravages of time belongs to the cathedral of Le Mans, and dates from the eleventh century. It depicts the Ascension with a sufficient interplay of color, an adequate fidelity to tone. It is still admired for its early excellence. But it does not approach the sharp delicacy, the gorgeous blending of shades, in the hundred and forty-three windows in the cathedral of Notre Dame at Chartres. Where on earth would you meet with windows that do?

In this cathedral named for her, the mother of Jesus participates with him in a glory of representations which the finest windows in the world ac-

cord them. The story of their life together, from
the Annunciation in Nazareth to their reunion in
heaven, progresses in a triumph of color, every shade
having a gemlike finish, in window after window.
The sequence begins with the angel in Mary's home.
It ends with her coronation, and everybody knows
what choirs are there to celebrate the occasion. The
coloring itself all but sings with joy.

To study the church windows anywhere on which
the glazier has lavished his art is to enjoy a resplendent survey in theology. With rich variety the designs symbolize the doctrines of faith, illustrate the
virtues, picture the sacraments being administered,
and portray important Biblical figures, a fair percentage of whom would have to be angels. The pictorial review might start off with the angels coming
to life from God and terminate with Christ coming
in glory with his angels on the Last Day. "The
windows of great cathedrals are all their meaning,"
an admirer was quite justified in writing. They speak
to the eye their homilies of tireless charm.

At Chartres, in point of fact, its brilliant windows
treat one thousand and three hundred subjects, and
contain almost four thousand figures. Just eleven
additional angels would have brought the sum to
that exact total. What a cathedral! What windows!

Staining glass reached its perfection in the thir-
teenth century, maintained it through the fourteenth,
then gradually lapsed into mediocrity when the

glazier became a mere tradesman. But in the nineteenth century, chiefly in Germany, the art recovered much of its lost proficiency. The windows in the cathedral of Glasgow, which came from Munich, may serve as a worthy example. The only trouble with them is, as Caryl Coleman has pointed out, that they clash with their environment. They are an obvious mismatch. They do not harmonize with the architecture.

But let it be said to the credit of the glass-stainer that, during the prolonged interval when his technique suffered a decline, he did not neglect the angels. They continued to flourish in his work. The stained windows of the Holy Cross Basilica in Florence may not show the consummate art of Donatello's stone-carved angel of the Annunciation or of Luca della Robbia's two angels crowning Mary their Queen, which are there in the shrine, but the windows do show the same lively interest in the heavenly court.

Nor did the wood carver slight the angel; especially not Tilman Riemenschneider. Here was a man whose piety intensified his art. His touch could bring a look of wonder into the wooden eye, and could fix a seeming flutter in the robes of his hovering angels. There is an aliveness in all his work done in wood, which his stone sculptures could not emulate.

He did equally well the isolated statue and the much more exacting task of sculpturing his figures to fit the designs of his own hand-carved altars. His supreme masterwork is one of these altars, done in his shop at Würzburg, and then moved to the church in Creglingen. It is all of wood. And it reveals a purity of art that cares for the slightest detail.

The altar features a tall triptych that rises from a broad base but narrows in successive stages to a tapering delicacy. As you approach it from a distance, this graceful narrowing of the frame conveys the impression of an upward surge, and already hints of the artist's theme before the statuary has had a chance to confirm it. The centerpiece, confirming it indeed at closer view, shows Our Lady ascending with effortless majesty in a cluster of angels. The side panels, representing the Annunciation and the Nativity and other Marian episodes, thus reinforce the theme. But that is not all. Our Lady of the Angels has not done with them yet. At the peak of the triptych, up where the tracery has grown ethereal, an angelic duo who await her arrival hold her crown between them, ready.

The whole triptych with its statuary groupings coheres admirably. Not a detail deviates. But what makes this masterwork an unusual fulfillment of theme is the suggestion of ascent which the entire wooden complex conveys.

Sculpture has produced angels of excellence out of every workable material known to the craft. An ivory triptych of *Madonna and Child with Angels,* which belongs to the Metropolitan Museum, looked good enough to make the front cover of a foremost national weekly in recent times. A terra-cotta miniature of St. Michael holding the scales of justice, which Andrea della Robbia carved for a lunette, has for delicacy of finish also become a favorite of its kind. Angels adapt themselves well to any material.

The modern sculptor, if he seems to have been overlooked, has not been. The truth of the matter is that, in comparison with the past abundance, his angels are scarce. But this does not mean they lack distinction. E. D. Palmer produced a statue of the *Angel of the Sepulchre* whose strong features reflect an authentic Easter glory. Alfred Gilbert achieved a notable triumph in his high relief of *Christ and Angels* which adorns the reredos of the cathedral in St. Albans, Hertfordshire. And that outdoor angel atop the apse of the cathedral of St. John the Divine in New York, who stands blowing his trumpet over the city, advertises to the metropolis the excellence of his sculptor. It was Gutzon Borglum who did that superb trumpeter.

No tourist to Colorado should think of returning home before going to see a modern angel that looks as if he could outspeed a jet. He will be found in the Catholic chapel at the Air Force Academy in

Colorado Springs. Appropriately, he shares the rear wall of the sanctuary with two other distinguished figures.

The painter and sculptor Lumen Martin Winter has covered that mural expanse with a glass abstract of the firmament. The mosaics are so inlaid as to represent the sky's changing shades of blue, turquoise, red, grey, and their blends. It is from this background, suggesting infinite space, that the three figures stand out in white-marble relief: an airborne dove with wings at ease, symbolizing the Holy Spirit; and to the left, in an ascent of glory, a most graceful Madonna in wind-blown robes, the patroness of aviators; while to the right, soaring at almost a horizontal angle, that swift-looking guardian angel of the air force.

To shape a block of marble, weighing one and a half tons, into such a lightsome beauty as that angel: this took plenty of doing. But the angel is worth every stroke of the effort. He is quite a flier.

Music Speaks for the Angels

IN TURIN stands the Marian shrine that St. John
Bosco planned under the guidance of its own
blessed patroness. He followed her directives. "I
began the building," he was to reveal years later,
"at her bidding and according to her instructions."
He had learned from Mary in visions what was to
be done. And he engaged an architect, Cavaliere
Anthony Spezia, to carry out her wishes.

The basilica includes a wealth of angels. Over
the main altar, to begin there, an enormous painting
of Mary and her Infant reveals in the extreme upper
area of the picture "a glimpse of heaven with choirs
of graceful little angels." So Eddie Doherty describes the cherubs in his biography of the saint.
But their melody only reaches the eye.

At the dedicatory service, let it be recalled from
an earlier reference, an all-girl choir of two hundred voices represented the angels. They did not
sing their hymns to Our Lady, Help of Christians,
unaided. They received plenty of assistance from
two flanks of male choristers: but the feminine
group, being the angels, had been stationed in the
center to dominate the harmony.

The music of the Mass, like the preliminary hymns, carried a motif of exultant joy. But there had been worked into it strong innuendos of something else: rumblings of past trouble which held a warning for the future. "People had listened to that music at the Mass," writes Doherty, "and swore they heard the sounds of battle in it — echoes of the guns at Lepanto and Vienna firing in defense of the Faith." It is a curious statement.

And it invites an explanation of the two bronze angels out on the belfries.

One of them holds in his proud grasp a banner. He lifts it prominently to view. He wants everyone down on the street to read its inscription: *Lepanto, 1571.* It would remind people of an acutely critical victory which the unarmed forces of a rosary crusade had achieved far rather than the hopelessly outnumbered warriors, who could not of themselves have prevailed. It would further remind, by its reference to a single instance, that Our Lady had time and again rescued the Faith from threats of imminent ruin.

The other angel holds a crown, extending it toward the statue on the dome, a statue of the Madonna, in design not unlike that of the interior painting. It is a fine gesture, a fine idea — though not Don Bosco's. The architect had taken a liberty with the plans. And the saint allowed it, cherishing so much as he did the queenship of Mary. But what the visionary had really prescribed for the second angel was again a dated banner to be held aloft. Its date was to be an incomplete one, however, with a dash to indicate the missing half. It would read simply, 19—.

The clairvoyance of St. John Bosco, well known to his generation, may have been forgotten in ours. It needn't be. His biographies have not gone out of print. And they all strongly suggest that, whatever he saw in vision, he knew from it that the Blessed Mother in her traditional role would once again through the providence of God intervene in some dreadful ordeal of the twentieth century to restore harmony in the end. "In the end," she has herself said at Fatima, "my immaculate heart will triumph."

If Don Bosco was denied the satisfaction of seeing in the angel's grasp that banner with its half date, at least the angel stood on the turret a witness to the queenship of Mary. And the saint was content to settle for that. He could scarcely have known the mildest disappointment when his basilica finally opened its doors to the faithful and, on June 9, 1868, resounded to the high jubilee of four hundred and fifty choristers. It pleased him to think, and to say, that two hundred of them were stand-ins for the angels.

Music relates well to the angels. It comes closer to doing justice to their flaming adoration than any other art. However these bodiless spirits convey the intense ardor of their nature, however they express to the All-Holy their insatiable love, music is the nearest thing to it that we know on earth. We know from Scripture.

The Bible cites no more favorite form of worship than "making melody to the Lord."[1] It recommends the practice with the urgency of a fixed idea. It not only urges us to sing with the angels; it does not hesitate to ask them to sing with us.

As the overjoyed find it a relief to their feelings to swing into a dance, a relief which ordinary walking could not bring, so does the Psalmist find it more to his inclination to sing than to say his prayers. He words them to a rhythm which, to be spoken, has to become a chant. "Sing to the Lord with thanksgiving; make melody to our God upon the lyre."[2] And not only upon the lyre! The Psalmist urges the use of the trumpet, of lute and harp, of timbrel and clashing cymbals, to accompany the chant.[3]

From this it becomes clear why the angels of religious art are such all-around musicians. They not only sing; they play stringed instruments, blow horns, clash cymbals. Hubert and Jan van Eyck in their *Lamb of God* altarpiece have painted an an-

---

[1] Eph. 5:19.

[2] Ps. 147 (146):7.

[3] See Ps. 150.

gelic choir on one open panel and on the other an angelic orchestra. Hans Burckmair in his picture of Christ the King, who is crowning his Mother Queen of Heaven, shows one of the attendant angels with a violin, another plucking the lyre, the third piping out a tune on the clarinet. And in Andrea della Robbia's group of statues which commemorates the same coronation, a quintet of angels are sounding off their trumpets in salute to their newly won Queen.

Scripture itself puts the most famous of trumpets, not yet heard, to the lips of an angel. The Lord in person, St. Paul writes, "will descend from heaven with a cry of command, with the archangel's call, and with the sound of the trumpet of God." It will be a rousing blast. "The trumpet will sound," the apostle again writes, this time to the Corinthians, "and the dead will be raised." "In that day," Isaiah makes the same prediction, "a great trumpet will be blown." And the evangelist Matthew sums up the testimony with saying of Jesus that "he will send out his angels with a loud trumpet call."[4]

In an attempt to identify the unnamed trumpeter of the Second Coming, tradition is divided between Gabriel and Michael. The stronger opinion favors the former since he is the angel of the Incarnation. Even profane literature is so inclined to believe. *Green Pastures* has no doubt of it. Nor has the

---

[4] 1 Thess. 4:16; 1 Cor. 15:52; Isa. 27:13; Matt. 24:31.

average allusion to the event. In *Life* magazine Franklin Russel ascribed to the whooper, an enormously large bird, "a cry like Gabriel's trumpet."

On the other hand, the prince of angels is not without a strong minority of backers. They are inclined to infer from certain Biblical allusions that he, by virtue of his dominance over evil, will be the one to blow that trumpet of doom. Didn't the angel Gabriel himself say of the last evil days that "at that time shall arise Michael"?[5] When the Lord sends out his angels to "gather his elect from the four winds,"[6] so the argument runs, who better than their original leader against Satan and his evil forces could lead the way? Cardinal Newman was of this persuasion. His hymn to St. Michael hasn't the slightest doubt who the great trumpeter would be.

The most admired reference to the trumpet of doomsday, outside Scripture, like Scripture does not name the angel. W. F. Wingfield has translated the tercet in question, from the *Dies Irae,* with an accuracy unsurpassed. Have a look at it:

> The mighty trumpet's marvellous tone
> Shall pierce through each sepulchral stone
> And summon all before the throne.

---

[5] Dan. 12:1.

[6] Matt. 24:31.

The angels are not strangers to the trumpet in Scripture. "Now the seven angels who had the seven trumpets," writes St. John of his auditory vision, "made ready to blow them."[7] And they each in turn did, in rousing salute to the Most High.

But the angels likewise know when to adore in silence. They can be good listeners. Art, taking the idea from liturgy and patrology, often portrays the angelic hush that attends the divine mystery of the altar. Of this, the Fathers of the Church have written at great length.

"Angels surround the priest," says St. John Chrysostom in a treatise on the priesthood. He speaks of their crowding around, bowing profounding, "worshiping him who lies on the altar." "Angels surround the priest when he is celebrating Mass," echoes St. Augustine. And St. Gregory the Great agrees that then "the heavens open and multitudes of angels come to assist at the Holy Sacrifice." The Fathers were always associating the Holy Eucharist with the angels. Yet nothing they ever wrote, and nothing else that art has ever done, has better understood that association than the wording and music of a single hymn. It is the incomparable *Panis Angelicus — Bread of Angels —* with its plea of such tender awe.

More often than not in the many hymns that sing of them, the angels themselves are singing. They

---

[7] Rev. 8:6.

sing in *Silent Night;* in *Jesus Christ Is Risen Today;* in, of course, *Angels We Have Heard on High;* and in *Holy God, We Praise Thy Name.* In *Adeste Fidelis — Come, All Ye Faithful —* they do not sing but at least are invited to sing to the Christ Child. Really, didn't the angels have the idea first?

The angel who announced the Savior's birth was only speaking: but crowds of the heavenly choir promptly appeared in the sky to sing to the world its first Christmas carol. And the best names in music have tried their utmost through the years to reproduce the magic of that moment. They made the attempt every time they set to work composing the Gloria of their numerous Masses.

Precisely how often was that? Who knows? Mozart alone did fifteen Masses. Gounod of *Ave Maria* fame did six. But why go on tediously enumerating? Suffice it to say that Beethoven and Haydn and Schubert and Bach have all given of their genius to the *Missa Cantata,* which has reproduced to the best of human ability the angelic Gloria over the plains of Bethlehem. Just the Gloria? No Mass is complete without its Sanctus, which these great composers again arranged into a harmony to fit the chant of the seraphim:

> Holy, holy, holy, Lord God of hosts.
> Heaven and earth are filled with your glory.
> Hosanna in the highest.

None of the immortals ever did a Mass superior to Bach's in B Minor. His technique holds the explanation. He accommodated his Gloria, his Sanctus, every other part of the sublime opus, to the tonal simplicity of the recurrent Gregorian interludes. He avoided the theatrical flairs to achieve a charming compatibility. "His monumental Mass in B Minor is, by common consent, one of the most magnificent creations ever evoked by the Christian Gospel," writes Jaroslav Pelikan of Yale University in *The Register*.

The professor further states that his fellow Lutheran "had a nightingale in his soul, and the nightingale was homesick for heaven."

Bach did feel a kinship with the angels. An English translation of Rüber's *Bach and the Heavenly Choir*, which appeared on the market in 1956, rightly associates the devout composer with a class of beings he cherished, revered, and hoped to spend his eternity with. If what a man ardently believes cannot but underlie his success, the angels have had no inconsiderable influence on the artistic development of Johann Sebastian Bach.

Of all the musical forms, the oratorio has proved the best qualified to give the angels their most glamorous treatment. *The Messiah* comes to mind at once. In it Handel leads up to the birth of Christ from a long succession of prophecies, granting to each the distinction of an entrancing solo with the constant interplay of a reaffirming chorus. As the predictions sharpen into particulars and a voice sings of a virgin conceiving and of a Child to be born a wonderful Counselor, mighty God, the Prince of Peace, the melodic accompaniment intensifies.

Thus the continual repetitions of the promise gather the momentum of a brewing storm until, at long last, the clamor breaks into a stunning lull and the angelic soloist is addressing the Virgin of Nazareth. The silence that attends the angel's every word to Mary is profound. It is also brief. For presently, in a frenzy of joy not to be restrained another moment, the chorus comes thundering in with its vehement echoes of the angelic announcement. It yields to a wild interchange of "he shall reign forever" and "of his kingdom there shall be no end" and a riotous interspersing of "forever and ever and ever" along with the most emphatic allelujas known to music.[8]

The choirs of Hood College and of the Naval Academy have on popular demand been doing an annual performance on television at Christmastide, rendering seasonal excerpts from *The Messiah:* and their audience is correctly made to feel that the growing intensity of the long prelude has but striven from the start to reach the Annunciation, which in turn opens another crescendo that mounts to a su-

---

[8] See Luke 1:26-33.

preme fulfillment when the Bethlehem skies are suddenly aflood with angelic jubilee.

Simultaneously with all this, one painting after another of the Virgin Mary, of Madonna and Child and the usual attendant angels, is shown on the screen to the rear of soloist and choir. It makes a helpful background. The music becomes the more deeply felt because of those vivid paintings from the masters, and the paintings the more touching because of that accompanying grandeur of sound. Nothing could better demonstrate the cooperation of the arts to their mutual benefit.

But *The Messiah,* while it accords the angels a major role, shows them in action only intermittently. It is Sir Edward Elgar's *Dream of Gerontius* that deals with them throughout. Cardinal Newman wrote the long poem first, before the music came, and of its forty-seven pages in the standard edition of his works the angels with hero Gerontius monopolize practically all of them. It was an extraordinarily difficult assignment for the music to fulfill the demands of so lofty a text. But it has measured up. The oratorio is by critical consent a triumph.

It opens with Gerontius on his deathbed. His faithful attendants in the room are praying, asking God for mercy on his soul, asking "all holy angels" to come to his aid. Gerontius himself implores his Savior to send him the angel of Gethsemane to ease

his agony. Faintly the dying man hears the priest
intone:

> Go, in the name
> Of Angels and Archangels; in the name
> Of Thrones and Dominations; in the name
> Of Princedoms and of Powers; and in the
>   name
> Of Cherubim and Seraphim, go forth!

An ineffable peace envelops the departing soul:

> I went to sleep; and now I am refresh'd.

> A strange refreshment: for I feel in me
> An inexpressive lightness, and a sense
> Of freedom, as I were at length myself,
> And ne'er had been before. How still it is!

There now breaks on Gerontius, enrapturing his
soul, his first vision and hearing of his guardian
angel, whose presence he has hitherto had to take
on faith:

> Now know I surely that I am at length
> Out of the body; had I part with earth,
> I never could have drunk those accents in,
> And not have worshipp'd as a god the voice
> That was so musical.

An angel whose every spoken word was such
music to Gerontius deserved to have a prominent
part in the oratorio, which to a generous degree he
has. Almost all of the oratorio consists of the conversation between the two. Their dialogue covers
that moment when the departed soul has arrived
in eternity and the angel accompanies it to its Particular Judgment. But there is no succession of time,
no going from one hour to the next, as on earth.
Intervals here, says the angel:

> Are measured by the living thought alone,
> And grow or wane with its intensity.

The recitatives, the arias, the choruses form a
composite of exquisite charm. The poetry exacts of
the music the loftiest effects, and receives them. His
sensations have for Gerontius the vividness of a
dream: but the dream is true.

He goes to judgment unafraid. His angel is with
him, telling him of the Judge:

> The sight of Him will kindle in thy heart
> All tender, gracious, reverential thoughts.
> Thou wilt be sick with love, and yearn
>   for Him.

The unpurified soul, at first glance, feels so un-
worthy of such Infinite Beauty that it willingly em-
braces its purgatory. Its sentence is self-inflicted.

It shrinks of its own choosing from the All-Holy
while in an agony of love it desires him. As the
angel says:

> And these two pains, so counter and so
>   keen —
> The longing for Him, when thou seest
>   Him not,
> The shame of self at thought of seeing
>   Him —
> Wilt be thy veriest, sharpest purgatory.

In *The Dream of Gerontius* the angels sing the
choruses, but only one of them has the finest arias.
With entrancing solicitude the guardian of Gerontius sings:

> Angels of Purgatory, receive from me
> My charge, a precious soul, until the day
> When, from all bond and forfeiture
>   released,
> I shall reclaim it for the courts of light.

Then, turning to Gerontius, he has the final word:

> Farewell, but not forever, brother dear;
> Be brave and patient on thy bed of sorrow;
> Swiftly shall pass thy night of trial here,
> And I will come and wake thee on the
>   morrow.

The audience that streamed out of Philharmonic Hall at Lincoln Center the night of February 20, 1968, when *The Dream of Gerontius* was playing there, were returning to a sad world. They had spent hours in an environment where love prevails and music is the natural form of speech. Yet the contrast need not have chilled in them the memory. If the message of the noble oratorio had got through to their minds, if they had the faith to receive it, they would have felt around them still the abiding solicitude of that better invisible world.

Music speaks for the angels. It speaks of them. It speaks to them. But best of all, it quotes them, melodizes their messages from God. Never, quite possibly, in its long history did it take an angel's words and make them sound so true to meaning as it did in Schubert's *Ave Maria*. A young composer who at twenty-eight could put such urgent tenderness into the utterance and yet keep it so sublime, ought to have the final tribute.

His melody sounds of paradise.

Angels in Classic Verse

CAN THERE BE an excess of angels in art? George Eliot raises the question. "Paint us an angel, if you can, with a floating violet robe, and a face paled by the celestial light," she allows, "but do not impose on us any esthetic rules which shall banish from the region of art those old women scraping carrots with their work-worn hands." The rebuke, while not disfavoring the angel, does not want him to monopolize art. It at any rate testifies to the angel's popularity.

Without its angels, many a masterpiece would lack fulfillment. How could a Schubert go about composing an *Ave Maria* if the song were not allowed to quote Gabriel? How could John Milton have produced his *Paradise Lost* if he had deleted from it every mention of Satan, of Michael, of its swarms of angels, good or bad? What would an admired group of statues mean to the outdoor crowds at Fatima, who see in it the memorial of an event, if the kneeling figures of the children about to receive Holy Communion were not faced by that standing figure of the angel with his ciborium?

These children who attracted the angel were of a lowliness to equal that of George Eliot's old women. Why should the author of *Adam Bede* have assumed, and spent a long Victorian paragraph developing the supposition, that the angel and the kitchen drudge do not mix and that art ought therefore to restrain its impulses in favor of the prosaic? As if the two were incompatible! Why need the treatment of one exclude the other? Guardian angels do not shun the lowly. And art knows it. The painter, the sculptor, the poet, have all portrayed the association.

"Thou bird of God!" Browning calls to the angel whose strong wings are poised over a praying child. The poet was describing a picture seen in an Italian chapel. And in his verse he wishes he could have an angel like that. He did have.

Newman did, too. But he had no doubt of his, addressing a prayer of faith to him:

> And mine, O Brother of my soul,
>   When my release shall come;
> Thy gentle arms shall lift me then,
>   Thy wings shall waft me home.

Lionel Johnson, starting off his poem, exclaims:

> O patron saints of all my friends!
> O guardian angels of them all!

Alice Meynell, absent from a friend and coun-

selor, takes comfort in the reflection that at least
their angels meet:

´   Who knows, they may exchange the kiss
        we give —
      Thou to thy crucifix, I to my mother?

"To some I have talked with by the fire," dreams
the poet Yeats — of angels, who else? And George
Gissing has supplied just the right words for the
mystic visionary whose experience the world sus-
pects: "Don't laugh! Don't any of you laugh; for
as sure as I live it was an angel stood in the room
and spoke to me. There was a light such as none
of you ever saw, and the angel stood in the midst
of it."

"Angels are bright still, though the brightest fell,"
condenses a whole chapter of theology. "Fools rush
in where angels fear to tread," exposes in a flash
what is not courage but madness. "In heaven an
angel is nobody in particular," shows Bernard Shaw
at his sardonic best. Angels have inspired many a
sharp epigram.

In a long poem celebrating Marlborough's victory
at Blenheim, Addison reaches its climax when all
in one stroke he acknowledges the power of an
avenging angel to wreak havoc, and acclaims the
hero just such a ministering agent of Providence:

> So when an angel, by divine command,
> With rising tempests shakes a guilty land
> (Such as of late o'er pale Britannia passed) ;
> Calm and serene he drives the furious blast,
> And, pleased the Almighty's orders to
>   perform,
> Rides in the whirlwind, and directs the
>   storm.

The fact that a tornado had of late ripped through the British Isles, as is mentioned, brought to the comparison a stunning immediacy.

Byron devotes an entire poem to the subject of angelic power. He took his facts from Scripture: "And that night the angel of the Lord went forth, and slew a hundred and eighty-five thousand in the camp of the Assyrians; and when men arose early in the morning, behold, these were all dead bodies."[1]

The army had been intent on capturing and enslaving Jerusalem. It had been warned. It didn't listen. It was wiped out.

The historians Josephus and Herodotus both affirm the event, even stating the number of the dead. They attribute the annihilation to a sudden plague of pernicious microbes. They could be correct. The angel, wreaking the vengeance of the Lord, could have infested the air with them; that is, he could have worked his purpose through natural means.

---

[1] 2 Kings (4 Kings) 19:35.

An angel elsewhere in Scripture is definitely reported to have smitten Herod Agrippa so that "he was eaten by worms and died."[2]

With or without the microbes, the job in Byron's poem as in the Bible, was quickly done:

> For the Angel of Death spread his wings
>   on the blast,
> And breathed in the face of the foe
>   as he passed;
> And the eyes of the sleepers waxed deadly
>   and chill,
> And their hearts but once heaved, and
>   for ever were still!

We must not think we have the world to ourselves. The angels, though belonging to the invisible world of the spirit, operate in ours. And of this, literature in whatever language speaks with conviction. Just as Sir Joshua Reynolds could not bring himself to paint St. Cecilia at the organ without having a group of cherubs listening in, so must Dryden get an attentive angel into his great ode written for Cecilia's feast day. Francis Thompson was not being at all exceptional in his reminder that:

> The drift of pinions, would we hearken,
> Beats at our own clay-shuttered doors.

---

[2] Acts 12:23.

Angels fly about in English verse as naturally as they do in St. John's apocalypse. If, in glancing around, the apostle "saw another angel flying in mid-heaven"[3] we can read of one in Milton hovering "with golden wings" and of a second gliding between the stars toward the earth:

> Down thither prone in flight
> He speeds, and through the vast ethereal sky
> Sails between worlds and worlds.

Even the poet Lovelace, confined to prison, but in his soul free, concludes his lyric with the triumphant boast that:

> Angels alone that soar above
> Enjoy such liberty.

And Browning, who had never been in prison and who rather found life on earth to his liking, dreams of a better freedom with "armies of angels that soar."

These flying beauties of poetry invite the illustrator to try his hand at them. His effort, always meaning well, does not always succeed. Belloc found the illustrations of Gray's *Elegy* in his childhood reader so many "Protestant angels brought up on milk pudding." They distracted him to mirth.

But the effort, when it comes from the master's hand, atones for the deficiences. Gustave Doré, the best-known illustrator of classic verse, owes much of his fame to his angels drawn for the *Divine Comedy* and *Paradise Lost*. His engravings of angels fulfill the descriptions that suggest them. His finesse shows an admirable fidelity. In selecting them to work on, he surely helped himself to God's plenty. In either epic they abound.

Paradise Lost has been described as "the dream of a Puritan fallen asleep over the first pages of his Bible." But the statement does not include enough. Milton's conception of the angelic war in heaven was suggested to him by the very last pages of his Bible. His mightiest episodes have for their authority a basic text from Revelation which tells of Michael and his angels rising up to fight and overthrow the evil cohorts of Satan.[4] Featuring man's fall from grace, the ambitious epic does well to consider the preliminary test of the angels, which was to have so strong a bearing on the human tragedy.

The doctrine of the Fall, with its insistence on freedom of will, the poet wisely has God the Father explain. Whose fault was it that man fell?

---

[4] See *ibid.* 12:7-8.

Whose but his own! Ingrate, he had of Me
All he could have; I made him just and
    right,
Sufficient to have stood, though free to fall.

And the angels had had the same freedom of choice:

Such I created all the ethereal Powers
And Spirits, both them who stood and
    them who fell.
... They themselves decreed
Their own revolt, not I. If I foreknew,
Foreknowledge had no influence on their
    fault.

The poet of the sonorous phrase finds abundant opportunity in his epic for exercising his talent. He glories in the vast choirs of the resplendent angels, from whose voices "uttering joy, heaven rang with jubilee, and loud hosannas filled the eternal regions." But, with his penchant for particulars, he can as easily turn from the multitude to the individual.

Of Michael, the princely hierarch, gliding toward Eden, the narrator relates:

The archangel soon drew nigh,
Not in his shape celestial, but as man
Clad to meet man.

And of him Adam observes to Eve:

> Such majesty
> Invests him coming: yet not terrible,
> That I should fear him, nor sociably mild,
> As Raphael, that I should much confide,
> But solemn and sublime.

The discriminate detail distinguishes *Paradise Lost.* Where could one ever find a sharper expression of the ache of loss which Adam feels in his estrangement from God than in his remembering aloud, as the archangel listens:

> On this mount He appeared; under this tree
> Stood visible; among these pines His voice
> I heard; here with Him at this fountain
>   talked.

Paradise Regained has proved to be a disappointing sequel. The momentum is not there to sustain the effort. Its verse cannot reach the exalted peaks which the occasions demand: such as the night, to cite an instance, when the sky broke into a glory of angels brighter than day and they sang to the shepherds. While the earlier poem has its letdowns, and too many of them, they are lapses from a high level; the narrative becomes clogged for the moment with extraneous material that serves no better purpose than to show off the poet's erudition; but

Paradise Lost always recovers, to rise to peaks of sublimity. *Paradise Regained* does not.

But it does continue, where *Paradise Lost* has left off, to commit to verse the long succession of angels known to the canonical Scriptures and the various Apocrypha. Taken together, the two productions supply just about the complete total. Milton wrote more abundantly of the angels than any other poet except Dante, yet with not nearly his quality.

John Milton, for all his narrative power, could not do character. His descriptions excel. His characterizations fail. Satan turns out to be his unintended hero, alongside whom the Almighty shrinks to something of an insufferable prig. The Miltonian good angel likewise inspires little admiration. But before Dante's angel, in the words of C. S. Lewis, "we sink in awe."

The angels from the *Commedia* do have about them a tremendous grandeur. Their voice or gesture, quite as much as their appearance, carries a dignity that would overpower — were it not so benign. The almost playful use of their wings, with which they amuse the reader, suggests invariably a strong-minded benevolence. But the proof of the statement lies in the testing, which any random sampling of the *Purgatorio* or the *Paradiso* will supply.

Arrived at the Sixth Cornice in their climb of Mount Purgatory, Dante and two companions heard a voice of such profound resonance that, as the poet admits, "I started just as a frightened, timid beast will do." It was an angel's voice, the dazzling angel who had come to direct the group through the Pass of Pardon.

> His aspect had bereft me of my sight;
> Wherefore I moved and stood behind my
>   mentors,
> Like one who guides himself by sound alone.
> And like the May breeze, herald of the
>   dawn,
> That gives out fragrance sweet with grass
>   and flowers,
> Suffusing, as it moves, the air about it —
> Such was the wind I felt upon my brow.
> Distinctly I could sense the moving pinions,
> And some ambrosial odor which they bore.

Feeling the breeze from them, the blinded straggler knew that those wings with a single flap could crush. Yet he had no fear, other than the fear that underlies awe. Nobody shies away from a scented May breeze.

In an earlier canto, when the weary climbers were looking for the dim stairway leading up to the Fifth Cornice, again an angel appeared out of the dark to guide them to it, and having done that, gave them a parting word with a gesture to make it unforgettable.

With outspread pinions gleaming like a
    swan's,
He who had thus addressed us showed
    the way
And turned us upward through the walls
    of rock.
Moving his wings, he fanned us, and
    affirmed
That those who mourn on earth are blest
    in heaven.

Dante, whose angels deserve their reputation, made much use of their wings. They do more than fly the angels around, or enhance their great beauty: they also, by an ingenuity of gesture, sharpen the meaning of their spoken word. Already at the First Cornice on the Mountain of Purgatory, Dante and Virgil got from its custodian a welcome that consisted of a single word — and a double gesture.

The glorious one approached, clad in white;
His countenance was like the morning star,
And trembled with a heavenly radiance.
He opened wide his arms, and spread
    his wings.
"Come," he said.

Did ever on earth a greeting of welcome have an accompaniment of such magnificent courtesy? But that is not all.

> He led us on to where the rock was cleft,
> And smote me with his wings upon the
>   brow,
> Promising that my passage would be safe.

Dante prefers to let their actions or gestures, quite as much as what they say, delineate his angels. Thus, to express their affinity to us and their regard for the virtuous soul, he has them crowd about Beatrice, rejoicing with her, showering upon her a wealth of flowers. For this once, the poet pays the angels no heed, hearing nothing of their chant. Nor does he catch the scent of the blossoms. His dream girl now glorified, unseen by him for a decade, holds his fascinated gaze:

> So eager were my eyes, and so intent
> To satisfy their ten long years of thirst,
> That all my other senses were extinct.

This foretaste of paradise was granted to Dante on the summit of Mount Purgatory. The vision, while a rapture of delight, was meant only to prepare him for the grand finale of his quest, the concluding canto of his long sustained effort, the summation of all that had gone before to make his imaginary journey through hell, purgatory and heaven the world's mightiest poem. Beatrice, personifying his strivings, was but a promise of the ultimate fulfillment.

Long before its final canto, to be sure, the *Paradiso*
has glowing references to the Beatific Vision. But
the poet does not see. He can only surmise from
the reaction of the angels to it. And this is tremendous. They move to a rhythm of tireless jubilee,
radiating their bliss in a splendor that grows ever
more glorious at every turn.

> Uttering a cry of such intensity
> That here on earth its like could not be
>   found:
> Its crashing thunder robbed me of all sense.

The Dantean cadence has no equal for describing
properly the jubilant choirs of God:

> . . . who, as they fly, behold
> And sing His glory, which enamors them;
> His goodness, which has given them such
>   glory.

If English blank verse conveys an adequate sense
of the grandeur, think of the greater effect of the
original tercets with their interlacing rimes in the
poet's own language. Yet it was more than his art
that achieved in so daring a poem its triumph of
utter credibility. It was Dante's faith in the truths
of the theme that imparted to his allegory such conviction and to his angels such unwavering magnitude.

His devils, the result of the same motivation, are relentless monsters of hate. You find nothing in their misuse of the will to admire. And that, as Ruskin observes, brings them closer to the scriptural truth than Milton's. They show a malevolence that has the intensity of rage when not subdued to the purposes of a cunning malice. They are horribly repulsive.

As with his angels of heaven, so with the demons of hell, Dante would have us judge them by their deeds. One of them, of a fiercely ugly appearance, caused the poet to shudder:

> Yet in his actions he was fiercer still.
> His wings were spread, his feet were light
>   and free;
> His pointed shoulder, which was square
>   and high,
> Was burdened with the haunches of a
>   sinner;
> His talons gripped the tendons, near the feet.

Action, including the pertinent gesture, Dante conveys with Homeric finality. The atmosphere of hell, with its perpetual stench, could not have been more impressively told than by what is said of the angel of God sent there on an errand:

> He slowly waved the murky air aside
> And ever moved his hand before his face.

This angel, forcing the devils to admit Virgil and Dante to the infernal city of Dis, does not tarry a moment beyond the demand of duty. The place disgusts him, and so he shows none of the leisurely courtesy which the poets were to receive from the angels of purgatory. The environment turned him somber.

If there is one quality that predominates in Dante and enhances every phase of his technique, Mark Van Doren has certainly hit upon it. "There has been no moment," he writes, "in Hell, in Purgatory, or in Paradise, when Dante's gaze at things has not been of that intense sort which Giotto painted on the faces, and indeed in the postures of his men and saints." This intensity of the poet was simply the ardor of his faith, which did not waver, and had for hell nothing but disgust, for heaven nothing but admiration. It put a fierce scorn into such lines as the following, which deride a former Paduan, now of hell:

> He twisted up his mouth, and like an ox
> That licks its nose, stuck out his loathsome
>   tongue.

Dante, the man of faith, having left the infernal regions, responded with high relief to the contrast in purgatory, where "our steps were measured by angelic strains" — for Dante and his poet companion had heard no singing in hell. He felt a shock of elation when, of a sudden, groping his way with his companion, "God's joyous angels shone before us." With an inexhaustible energy of response he thrilled to the pronouncement made grander by the sight of Beatrice, herself a radiant focus of glory, as she told of the innermost secret of "heaven which is pure light; light of understanding full of love; love of true good full of joy; joy that surpasses every sweetness."

And when in a stirring finale the poet heard the high festival of the blessed, all the angels and all the saints praising together the Source of their bliss, the intensity which he had maintained from the start did not desert his special need of it now.

"Unto the Father, Son and Holy Ghost,"
All Paradise began to sing, "be glory" —
So that the strains inebriated me,
And what I saw before my eyes now seemed
To be a smile of all the universe:
For I was drunk with joy of sight and sound.
O bliss! O happiness ineffable!
O life, made whole with perfect love and
  peace!
O riches, leaving nothing for desire!

Our Spiritual Cousins

THE LADY who sits down to a good dinner does it because she is, in blunt truth, just another hungry animal. She does not get down on her knees to eat, as the moose does; or jump about to aid digestion as the frog does; or break into tears while chewing her food, as the masticating crocodile does (unless the food be too highly peppered). But as surely as they do and the angel doesn't, she eats.

One fact leads to another, and to a dozen new distinctions. There is no end to the amusement. While the elephant prefers to sleep standing up and people for the purpose take to their beds, although the somnambulist walks around, the angel doesn't sleep at all. Whereas the octopus has been known to turn pink and a person to blush a deeper shade under emotional stress, the angel, who lives more intensely than either, remains a colorless spirit. The differences are there, and the similarities, between us and the animals: and the contrasts tickle our curiosity.

But the differences between us and our spiritual relatives, balanced against the similarities, afford a worthier study.

Angelology ought to rank higher as a study than either anthropology or zoology; it deals with higher beings. And the fact of its being dismissed as of no account or so much guesswork may be laid to a prejudice. "We have more real knowledge about the angels than about the brutes," Newman insists in one of his more famous sermons, *The Invisible World.* Do we actually know, runs his argument, whether these animals think or not? What their destiny is? But Scripture has not left us in the dark about the angels.

In his *All Things Considered,* this very idea is one of Chesterton's deeper but mirthful considerations. He says: "A turkey is more occult and awful than all the angels and archangels. In so far as God has partly revealed to us an angelic world, He has partly told us what an angel means. But God has never told us what a turkey means. And if you go and stare at a live turkey for an hour or two, you will find by the end of it that the enigma has rather increased than diminished."

Resembling the beast, yet comparable to the angel, we are an intermediate between them. Against the Manichean horror of flesh, the Fourth Lateran Council decreed the human body respectable. Man, who hungers for the stars, need not feel ashamed of his appetite for bread. But it is this duality about him that intrigues. We can growl like a dog. Yet, like a seraph, we pray.

What distinguishes us from the animal relates us to the angel. It makes him our cousin. We have the brains to think as really, if not so powerfully, as he does. We have his ability, though to a lesser degree, to love. Our future lies with him: his world is our destiny. The affinity could by any number of such parallels be demonstrated. But nothing more convincingly proves it than our understanding with him the meaning of words. The fox would make nothing of our lessons in grammar. None of the angels would need them.

In their reported apparitions they proved themselves to be the readiest of linguists. They did not grope for words. No language was foreign to their intelligence. They commanded an easy diction. Their vocabulary never failed them.

The angel who appeared to Joseph of Nazareth had no trouble making himself understood in Aramaic. The angel who spoke Syrian to St. Simeon Stylites did so fluently. The angel who conversed with St. Lydwina had to know Dutch, which he did. The angel who would day after day visit the home of St. Margaret of Cortona to give her lessons in the spiritual life gave them in an Italian that never faltered.

But all this pertains to the angels' conversing with saintly people in their many apparitions to them. How do these heavenly spirits exchange thoughts among themselves? That they do, Scripture implicitly affirms. Gabriel, of the overpowering voice, suggested in his message to the prophet Daniel an understanding between himself and the archangel Michael. Each would seem to have known the other's motives.[1]

Was it by a kind of mental telepathy? Theology has its own word for it, *illumination*. Angels by a mere act of the will, St. Thomas Aquinas explains, open their minds to reveal to one another whatever ideas they choose to impart. Thus, quick as a lightning flash, Satan made known to his fellow angels his threat upon the Almighty. They caught his meaning instantly, some of them enticed by it, the majority not. Stung by its absurdity, Michael sprang into action to lead the faithful with a war cry that was to become his name — *Who is like God?*

The angelic interchange of ideas, being direct, instantaneous, illuminative, excels the human. We are compelled to express our minds through an imperfect medium. Every language has its deficiencies which more or less becloud the meaning. Besides, the speaker himself may have an insufficient vocabulary, or the hearer may have for idioms little sensitivity. Any of these liabilities will detract from a precise communication of thought. Worse yet, when a liar speaks, his words do not convey his thought. They deceive.

---

[1] See Dan. 10:13.

Illumination, on the contrary, never does. Satan, whom Christ has called the father of lies,[2] seduced the other fallen angels, not because they did not read his mind correctly but because they did. His lie consisted in denying the truth of God's supremacy in favor of his self-acclaimed superiority, which was totally false. But his evil followers, aware of these thoughts in his perverse mind, which reflected and outshone the pride in theirs, preferred their own rebellion to a subserviency under God. They caught the devil's meaning all right: he would be their leader.

A similar influence exists among the faithful angels. A member of a higher choir, having superior intelligence, may illuminate one of lower rank to a greater knowledge of God. Every angel has his grade of excellence and within that his individuality. There is a continual intercommunication among the angels. "They exchange between them without words their thoughts, their counsels," writes St. John Damascene.

But it is what the angels have in common, their beatitude, that puts to best use their exchange of thought. All of them, loving God together as the Source of their being, cannot but love themselves and one another in their beatific vision of him. They see in his infinite beauty their own finite reflection,

---

[2] John 8:44.

forever admiring one another accordingly, expressing their admiration in a joy of spirit which the sublimity of great music gives us some faint idea of. The angelic choirs, united in God, are a vast admiration society which includes the blessed from our own world. We are relevant to the angels, and they to us.

That we attribute to them a voice like ours, when in reality they speak to one another without words, is only to make ourselves realize the truth of their doing it at all. They did, of course, in addressing their visionaries on earth, adopt a human voice. And it always had the greatest charm. The eulogist who said of Martin Luther King that he spoke with the tongue of angels was paying the slain orator a superlative compliment.

St. Paul originated the phrase, to be sure, saying that if one should speak with the tongue of angels and have not charity, it would be a waste of breath.[3] All that fine eloquence, the best there is, could not make up the loss. It was high praise for the virtue from a man who knew how an angel could talk. He was not imagining. The apostle had on board ship heard one.

The saints knew a great deal about the angels. They were on the best of terms with these spiritual cousins who were constantly and visibly doing them

---

[3] See 1 Cor. 13:1.

favors. St. Stanislaus Kostka, detained in a hostile residence where he lay dying, received Holy Viaticum from an angel. Frances of Rome once found in her home a visiting angel who appealed to the mother in her because he didn't look a day older than eight years, although the saint must have known that the heavenly boy was in reality older than the world. St. Rose of Lima, whose angel used to converse with her and call her intimate names, would sometimes have the satisfaction of seeing him appear just in time to open the front-yard gate to her approach when she would return home from her walks. Talk about service!

But the saints were privileged characters. We shall never completely know, I suppose, what favors the angels bestowed on them — especially in the more desperate emergencies. If St. Gemma's angel ran errands for her, he also on the night that she received the stigmata was there in visible form to assist her. "I felt pain in my hands and feet and side," the saint, then twenty-two, has revealed; "and when I arose I noticed they were dripping blood. I covered them as best I could and, with my angel's help, managed to climb into bed."

It astonishes us that the martyrs could have endured their agonizing torments so heroically, without complaint. We should have less cause to be puzzled if we took more seriously the statements which those of them were able to give out, for our enlightenment, during the intermissions of their prolonged torture.

"Didn't you feel those dreadful cruelties?" St. Theodosius was asked during such an interruption, when it looked as if he suffered nothing.

"At first I did," he replied. "But quickly an angel was there to refresh my aching wounds. And when the tortures stopped I was sorry, because then the angel disappeared and I no longer enjoyed his sweet presence."

Rufinus has verified the report. It is nothing unusual. The chronology of the martyrs is replete with like instances. St. Lawrence, St. Vincent of Lisbon, St. Venantius, St. Agnes, St. Dorothy, St. Cecilia, St. Eulalia, some of them scarcely more than children, all had their angels to comfort them: to induce in them such intensity of joy from the beauty of their presence that the torment no longer mattered. St. Teresa of Avila, who ought to know, once said that a mere moment of mystic experience so overwhelms the soul and impresses the memory that suffering loses its dread. Her own cheerful life of suffering indicates the sincerity of her statement, which the death of the martyrs confirms.

Angels intervene in human life because, by God's will, they consider our business theirs. They mind it better than we can. And to their favorites, the saints, they have by their apparitions given evidence of their concern.

By their apparitions they have done more. They have proved that the human form is not beneath their dignity, and is worthy of paradise. The angels show off the human body, when they assume one, with a glory not of this world. Need that surprise? Heavenly glory does happen to be its potential destiny.

We share with the angels an advantage over the rest of creation. As much animal as the caged curiosities of the zoo, we are yet their superiors — or they wouldn't be there. It is a superiority that transcends the whole material universe.

Flowers have been created, not to delight themselves, but to delight us; it is not for them to notice their beauty, feel their charm, or to study botany; the prerogative is ours. Wheat grows out of a tiny seed, ripens toward its harvest without knowing of the process; its fertility takes no pride in supplying our human need for bread; it is we who admire the accomplishment. A cow by her own inner chemistry no less remarkably transforms clover into milk; the wonder of which, however, escapes her; she must leave to us the wonder as well as yield to us the cream. And so it goes, from the least to the greatest in the whole range of materialities.

None of them has the human intelligence, far less the angelic, to think of their Creator. The law of gravity doesn't know that it holds the stars to their course, controls the traffic of the spheres, to advertise his omnipotence. As for those very stars, the magnificence of which overawes astronomy, they could never for as long as they shine understand the sentiments they once aroused in a poet many generations ago. Unable to keep the rapturous truth to himself, he sang out to the God of the universe:

> When I behold your heavens, the work of
>   your fingers,
> the moon and the stars which you have
>   set in place,
> what is man that you should be mindful
>   of him,
> or the son of man that you should care
>   for him?

And the psalmist concludes:

> You have made him little less than the
>   angels,
> and crowned him with glory and honor.[4]

Christ himself has proclaimed the high status possible to us: our association with the angels. He once did so in answer to "some Sadducees, those who say that there is no resurrection." They had asked an insidious question. They got from him no uncertain statement about the faithful departed:

---

[4] Ps. 8:3-5 (according to the wording of the Vulgate).

"They cannot die any more because they are equal to angels."[5]

The woes that flesh is heir to cannot tarnish the glory of such a destiny. We are worms, Dante would remind us, who have it in our power to become the angelic butterfly. And James H. Billington, in a scholarly analysis of what ails modern education, because of its divorcement from spiritual values, concludes with a Dantean statement of his own: "Man is a fallen angel as well as a naked ape."

Related to both, he is, however, closer to the angel. His future is not with the animal world. He belongs by destiny, in the golden words of St. Augustine, to "the holy and august assembly of angels, the republic of heaven, in which God's will is law."

Dostoevsky once said with utter contempt for those dreamers who seek on earth their paradise: "All the Utopias will come to pass only when we grow wings and people are converted into angels." The remark ought to be heeded by an age that worships its own frenzied contemporaneity to no very evident satisfaction. It is a gem of wisdom from a man of faith, who believes that Christ's kingdom is not of this world and that, only when the wayfarer of earth has joined the fellowship of angels, shall the worthy exile have come home at last.[6]

---

[5] Luke 20:27, 36.

[6] See John 18:36; Matt. 25:34.

"May the choirs of angels welcome you," the funeral chant addresses the soul of the deceased, whose mortal remains will on the final day revive to be happily reunited to the soul, if that soul has attained salvation. It will indeed be the happiest of reunions. It will be for the glorified body a proud homecoming, with all the angels in attendance, as the Christ of their adoration himself pronounces the welcome: "Come, O blessed of my Father, inherit the kingdom prepared for you."[7]

---

[7] Matt. 25:34.

CHAPTER NOTES

The quotations not otherwise identified in THE ANGELS IN RELIGION AND ART are from the sources here listed. The folios in parentheses indicate the pages in this book in which the quotations are to be found.

Chapter I: Dorothy Sayers, Introduction to her translation of the *Purgatory,* Vol. II of *The Comedy of Dante Alighieri* (p. 1); Thomas Wolfe, *Look Homeward, Angel* (p. 1); Somerset Maugham, *A Writer's Notebook* (p. 1); Cardinal Newman, *Discourses to Mixed Congregations* (p. 2); Dante, Canto II of Lawrence Grant White's translation of the *Inferno,* in *The Divine Comedy* (p. 2); the phrase "an angel in a frock," Frederick Locker-Lampson, "My Mistress's Boots" (p. 3); Shakespeare, *Cymbeline* (p. 3) and *Romeo and Juliet* (p. 3); Keats, "The Eve of St. Agnes" (p. 3); John Ashe, "Meet No Angels, Pansie" (p. 4); George Gordon, Lord Byron, *Don Juan,* Canto II (p. 4); Erasmus, letter to Ulrich von Hutten (p. 4); Ronald Knox, panegyric delivered at Chesterton's funeral, reprinted in *Occasional Sermons* (p. 4); John Butler Yeats, in a letter to his elder son, the poet, quoted in *The Man from New York: John Quinn and His Friends,* by B. L. Reid (p. 5); the phrase "Fair sister of the seraphim," Richard Crashaw, "The Flaming Heart" (p. 5); Wordsworth, "A Phantom of Delight" (p. 5); Aldous Huxley, *After Many a Summer Dies the Swan* (p. 6); Charles Dickens, *David Copperfield* (p. 6); Robert Louis Stevenson, title essay in *Virginibus Puerisque* (p. 6); Cole Porter, "True Love" (p. 8); Mary Thayer, "The Weeks That Changed the White House," *McCall's,* January, 1968 (p. 11).

Chapter II: Hilaire Belloc, *Survivals and New Arrivals* (p. 12); Jacques Maritain, *The Peasant of the Garonne,* translated by Michael Cuddihy and Elizabeth Hughes (pp. 15, 16); Dante, Canto XXXI of White's translation of the *Purgatorio* in *The Divine Comedy* (p. 21); *TV Guide,* May 25-31, 1968, issue, p. 46 (p. 22).

Chapter III: St. Thomas Aquinas, *Opusculum* 60, I (p. 26); St. Thomas, *Summa theologica,* Pars I (p. 27).

Chapter IV: John Keats, *Lamia,* Part II, line 231 (p. 40).

Chapter V: St. Ambrose, *Hexaemeron,* I, 5, 19 (p. 44).

Chapter VI: Milton, *Paradise Lost,* Book I, lines 250-256 (p. 52); and Book I, lines 261-263 (p. 53); Ronald Knox, *A Retreat for Beginners* (p. 55); *Summa theologica,* Supp., Q. 70, Art. 3 (p. 55).

Chapter VIII: Canto II of Henry F. Cary's translation of the *Purgatory,* in *The Divine Comedy of Dante Alighieri* (p. 70); St. Augustine, *Enchiridion,* 58 (pp. 71-72); Pope St. Gregory, *Hom. 34 in Evang.* (p. 73); Dante, *Paradiso,* Canto III (p. 77).

Chapter XI: St. Jerome, *In Matt.,* 18, 10 (p. 97); St. Basil, *Hom. in Ps.,* 33, 5 (p. 97); St. Anselm, *Elucid.,* II, 31 (101); St. Ambrose, *In Ps.* 37: 43; 38: 32 (p. 103); St. Bernard, *In Ps.* [Ps. 90: 11], Sermo XII (p. 103).

Chapter XII: Cardinal Newman, *Essays on Miracles* (p. 117). The material about Dr. Alexis Carrel is from his *Man the Unknown,* p. 148 (p. 118).

Chapter XIII: John Milton, *Lycidas,* line 161 (p. 126).

Chapter XV: Dante, Canto X of Lawrence Grant White's translation of the *Purgatorio* (p. 141); George Gordon, Lord Byron, *Don Juan,* Canto III (p. 142); Edwin Muir, "The Annunciation" (p. 143); Ronald Knox, commentary in *The Epistles and Gospels for Sundays and Holydays* (p. 155).

Chapter XVI: Dorothy Sayers, *The Nine Tailors* (p. 158); Gilbert Keith Chesterton, "The Stone Masons," in *The Wild Knight and Other Poems,* and Chesterton,

Tremendous Trifles (p. 160); Hilaire Belloc, *The Path to Rome* (p. 163).

Chapter XVII: *Dies Irae,* translation according to W. F. Wingfield, in *The Hymns of the Breviary and Missal,* ed. Britt (p. 173); St. John Chrysostom, *On the Priesthood,* VI, 4 (p. 174); St. Augustine, quoted in *All about the Angels,* by E. D. M. (p. 174); St. Gregory the Great, *Dialogi* IV, 58 (p. 174).

Chapter XVIII: Robert Browning, "The Guardian Angel" (p. 184); Cardinal Newman, "Guardian Angel" (p. 184); Lionel Johnson, "Friends" (p. 184); Alice Meynell, "Thoughts in Separation" (p. 185); Joseph Addison, *The Campaign,* lines 282-287 (p. 186); Byron, "The Destruction of Sennacherib," lines 9-12 (p. 187); Francis Thompson, "The Kingdom of God" (p. 187); Milton, *Paradise Lost,* Book V, lines 266-268 (p. 188); Richard Lovelace, "To Althea from Prison" (p. 188); Hilaire Belloc, letter to Mrs. Wansbrough, dated Jan. 6, 1927, quoted in *The Life of Hilaire Belloc,* by Robert Speaight (p. 188); *Paradise Lost,* Book III, lines 97-99, 100-101, and 116-118; Book IX, lines 238-240, and 232-236; Book IX, lines 320-322 (pp. 190, 191); C. S. Lewis, Preface to *The Screwtape Letters and Screwtape Proposes a Toast* (p. 192); Dante, Cantos XXIV, XIX, XII, and XXXII, respectively, of White's translation of the *Purgatorio* (pp. 193, 194, 195); Cantos XXI and XXXI of White's translation of the *Paradiso* (p. 196); Cantos XXI, IX, and XVII of his translation of the *Inferno* (pp. 197, 198); Cantos XXXII and XXVII of his translation of the *Purgatorio* (pp. 198, 199); Canto XXX of Arthur John Butler's translation of *The Paradise of Dante Alighieri;* Canto XXVII of White's translation of the *Paradiso* (p. 199).

Chapter XIX: St. John Damascene, *De fide orthodoxa,* II, 3 (p. 204); Dante, Canto X of the *Purgatorio* (p. 210); James H. Billington, "The Humanistic Heartbeat Has Failed," *Life,* May 24, 1968 (p. 210); St. Augustine, *De civitate Dei* (p. 210).